The Teaching Assistant's Gu

Also available from Continuum

The Teaching Assistant's Guide to Dyspraxia

Geoff Brookes

continuum

Continuum International Publishing Group

The Tower Building	80 Maiden Lane
11 York Road	Suite 704
London, SE1 7NX	New York, NY 10038

www.continuumbooks.com

British Library Cataloguing-in-Publication Data
A catalogue record for this book is available from the British Library.

ISBN: 9-780-8264-9760-4 (paperback)

Typeset by Kenneth Burnley, Wirral, Cheshire
Printed and bound in England by Antony Rowe Ltd, Chippenham, Wilts

Contents

This book is dedicated to my son David,
who inspired me.
He still does.

Foreword

Let's start at the end. It may seem perverse but there's a reason. Let's look at what can happen when the time at school is over.

My son David has dyspraxia. It has been his burden and many people have helped him to carry it. I couldn't make it go away. No one could. So we all had to learn to deal with it.

While he was at school, the staff there (Morriston Comprehensive School in Swansea) did a lot to help him. They learned a lot about dyspraxia too. An important part of what they did was to apply for and administer extra time for David during formal examinations like GCSEs, AS and A levels. It all went very well. It took a great deal of pressure off him and he was able to perform very well. He got the (high) grades he needed to study Law at Reading University. Everyone was delighted. Triumph over adversity.

So he went along during Fresher's Week to register for the same kind of support he'd had in school. When he arrived, there were so many seeking support for their dyspraxia that they had to organize three separate meetings.

There is a lot that we can learn from this little tale.

First of all, it is clear that people now are much more confident about identifying, and admitting to, dyspraxia. It isn't always hidden away any more. Dyspraxia has always been there, of course, but it has often been marginalized where it hasn't been denied altogether.

But it isn't regarded as a made-up condition any more. It has its own websites and organizations and crusaders. And there are things we can do about it, things that make a difference.

So let's do them.

The other thing, of course, is that this story shows that dyspraxics can, and should, achieve if they receive appropriate help. The evidence is here. Universities are full of them.

So when you find yourself dealing with dyspraxia, don't ever think that it doesn't matter. You are not simply ticking off the lessons until you can go home. You really can make a huge difference.

In my experience dispraxics are very intelligent people who have an irritating barrier to overcome. You will be able to help them through it or around it. With the right sort of support and space that you will be in a position to provide, then children with dyspraxia will achieve. You will be able to take enormous pleasure in their achievements because of the contribution you will have made.

In fact, perhaps more than in many other conditions, the close and focused attention of an adult will be the most significant contribution.

You can and should be that adult. It is a job you will enjoy.

So enjoy.

Instructions

As you read this book you will find 26 different development activities scattered throughout it. They are designed to give you the opportunity to develop your own knowledge based upon your own particular experiences. They are there to encourage you to think about what you are doing and to enable you to draw conclusions that will help you. In addition, in order to act as a prompt to this process, I have included issues you might like to consider as you read, in the boxes called 'Think for a moment . . .'

The intention is that you will become an active, not passive, reader through the way in which the material has been structured. I hope you find this a helpful approach.

Development activities

1. Existing knowledge
2. Observation
3. Vocabulary
4. Comparisons
5. Sensitivity
6. Families
7. Review
8. Checking records
9. Our obligations
10. Supporting parents

Let us begin

When I sat down to write this book, I stopped to consider what you might know about this condition. If I had been writing this book a few years ago, I would have said that you knew nothing. Today I am inclined to say, 'At least something'. Awareness about dyspraxia is growing all the time. When my son was diagnosed with dyspraxia, there was little available to tell us what it actually implied. There is much more available today, thank goodness.

The first thing to say is that we haven't just invented it. It has always been there, but the symptoms and consequences were not properly brought together in one coherent diagnosis. We should be pleased that it has been identified, for the condition is a real one, with a past and certainly with a future.

Dyspraxia has been called many things in its time. Technically it should really be referred to as Developmental Co-ordination Difficulty, but for the purposes of this book I shall use the term dyspraxia.

It is certainly a term that is being used far more frequently. It is a condition that calls upon the attention of so many differently skilled professional specialists. It is not a straightforward condition. And you must never say that it is rare.

Think for a moment . . .

Why did you decide to read this book?

What did you hope to get out of it?

Making contact with dyspraxia

I have no doubt whatsoever that, as a teaching assistant, you will come into contact with dyspraxia. Indeed it is possible that you might be the professional who actually diagnoses it. Someone at some point has to bring all the information together and that person might well be you.

Dyspraxia refers to the way in which the brain works in a different and less precise way for some people than it does for others. And no one really knows why this should be. There are specific circumstances in which dyspraxia can be acquired, particularly by older people, but developmental dyspraxia cannot be explained by events like a brain injury. It is there for no apparent reason. All you can say is that the organization of the brain is highly inefficient. The pathways that messages take within it are disrupted or impaired. It isn't any more complicated than that. But the implications are far-reaching.

Of course, there are those who claim that they do understand where it comes from and, more importantly, who claim to be able to offer cures, but I am afraid that at the time of writing (January 2007) there is little substance for such claims. If you have it, then deal with it.

We are unable to re-wire the connections. We can wait for them to grow or wait for the messages to find a different way to their destination, but there is nothing you can do to get rid of it. Once you've got it, you must learn to live with it.

In most cases the condition can be managed, as long as it is approached with awareness and sympathy. These qualities are vital and remind us what the role of the teaching assistant should be, though that isn't really that much different from the role of any adult in a school.

Awareness and sympathy

Awareness and sympathy do not always spring naturally within the jungle of the playground. Dyspraxics will be hurt by the unthinking cruelty of some of their peers. Because they seem odd, they will suffer. But you can provide the support and the listening space that they need. You are ideally suited to this role. You are not a teacher, yet you sometimes behave like one. This gives you authority and your role, which is often highly child-focused, can also make you approachable and non-threatening.

If you are going to offer help and strategies, then you have got to know something about the condition. A little technical knowledge will help you a great deal. As knowledge about the brain and how messages are carried within it grows, so does our understanding of what happens when things go wrong. It is impossible to define what is normal within something as rich and complex as the brain, but certainly the dyspraxic child has identifiable difficulties that the rest of us would not want to share.

But I hope this book will show you that there are many opportunities for positive outcomes. And while it is important to understand where the condition comes from, putting teaching assistants in a position where they can provide effective support and guidance is what this book is all about. You need to be informed about the condition and, more importantly, acquire the strategies to provide effective help to the dyspraxic learners that you meet. They are special children. They have so much that they can offer. They have talents, determination, and a different way of looking at the world. Theirs is a vision that we would be wrong to sacrifice.

They need our help if they are to make the kind of contribution that they should. As professional and committed adults, the staff in the school, whatever their role, must offer that help. The fact that you are prepared to read a book such as this is an indication of your commitment and your desire to make a significant contribution to the place where you work.

I want you to end your research into dyspraxia with an increased level of sympathy and understanding for the dyspraxic learner. Because those are precisely the sort of responses that will ensure a better provision and school experience for dyspraxics everywhere.

Understand, sympathize, support. This is exactly what dyspraxics need.

By achieving an increased level of understanding, you will be able to offer important help to children and students who really need it. In such a way you will be able to develop true effectiveness and, also, lasting job satisfaction.

Development activity 1: Existing knowledge

By asking your colleagues at all levels, from top to bottom, find out how much they actually know about dyspraxia.

Do they know what it is?

Do they know about its implications?

Do they know who has it?

Do they know what to do about it?

1

What is dyspraxia?

Before we go any further, we need to establish what we are actually talking about when we refer to dyspraxia.

Developmental dyspraxia is a neurologically based disorder. This means it happens inside the brain where we cannot see it. This is the first and greatest problem. We cannot see it. It isn't visible like a broken leg. But we know it is there from the tell-tale signals that it gives us. It is a difficulty with motor planning that isn't acquired through injury or accident. It is present from birth. When the pack was shuffled, the dyspraxic child was dealt a joker. Sorry about that. Nothing we can do.

The Dyspraxic Foundation in 1999 offered a useful definition of what it is. They said that it is 'an impairment or immaturity in the organisation of movement which leads to associated problems with language, perception and thought.' And even though we can define it, all we can ever do is to deal with the consequences of the condition. There is nothing that can be done to prevent it or to make it go away. We can't remove a component and replace it. There is significant disruption to the things that a person is trying to do, because the paths that the messages take within the brain are longer and more convoluted that they are in the brains of the rest of us. Dyspraxic subjects will take longer to respond to the things around them. They will have a poor understanding of the messages that their senses convey, and experience some difficulty in turning those messages into appropriate actions. Physical activities are hard to learn and hard to remember. No one else can ever truly understand what it is like to live within a dyspraxic brain, but it must be like reaching out for something which is always tantalizingly just out of reach or trying to pick up jelly wearing rubber gloves.

Think for a moment . . .

The delays in the brain are not hours or minutes. They are tiny, but significant. What do you think the consequences of such delays might be?

The motor cortex

With dyspraxia it appears that parts of the motor cortex in the brain don't develop properly. This prevents messages from being transmitted efficiently from the brain to the body. So dyspraxics have difficulty in planning movement to achieve a predetermined idea or purpose. They want to catch the ball, but they cannot arrange their body with sufficient efficiency in order to do so. Their hands are still coming together after the ball has smacked them in the mouth. I am sure we have all seen people like this in our time, and in the great scheme of things it is mightily unimportant. But there are other areas of life where disruption to messages can have far-reaching implications. Try to imagine the consequences, for example, of inefficient message transmission in the emotional aspects of your life. It can make things very fraught indeed, because your ability to read others will be seriously impaired. We often respond to people instinctively, and yet a dyspraxic's responses are slightly delayed. They don't therefore respond like the rest of us.

To sum it all up, the dyspraxic child cannot make their body do what they want it to do quickly enough. Actions can be carried out but not instinctively and with little conviction. They cannot be repeated with any reliability or success. If you think of the brain as an electrical circuit, then connections appear to be either missing or disrupted. This can be extremely frustrating.

Inside the brain

Three things happen inside the brain.

1. *Ideation.* This is when we form the idea of employing a movement we already know about to achieve a planned purpose.
2. *Motor planning.* This is when we plan the action needed to achieve this idea.
3. *Execution.* This is when we carry out the planned movement.

A child with dyspraxia will know what they need to do, but is unable to make the thing happen as effectively as the rest of us.

So a child might be unable to reproduce mouth movements efficiently. Thus if they were asked to put their tongue in their cheek, they would be unable to carry out the instruction, even though they would be able to do it unconsciously. They can do it but they are not sure of how they can make it happen. This prevents a child from moving in a planned way. They know that they want to kick a ball but they cannot organize the necessary movements to achieve this. The ball has long since moved away before they can arrange their leg to swing in its direction.

Anyone working in a school must recognize that it can affect any or all areas of development – sensory, physical, intellectual, emotional, social or language. And this lack of efficiency in delivering and receiving messages can happen in any of the millions of connections within the brain. Every dyspraxic person is different as a result.

Development activity 2: Observation

Think carefully about the learners you meet around the place where you work.

Make a discreet list of those who seem to exhibit some of the characteristics we have identified so far.

Observe them carefully over a period of time.

What evidence have you identified?

What do their existing records reveal about them?

Have they been diagnosed as dyspraxics already?

Do you need to alert someone else about what you have seen?

2

Thinking about how the brain works

This is a difficult idea, because most of us never think about how the brain works. It just does, and for most of us it is just as well that it can sort this out for itself. But if we are going to make some progress in establishing an understanding of what this condition is about, then we will have to spend a little time thinking about how we think. In this way dyspraxia will reveal itself.

It helps if we know, in general terms anyway, how the brain works in normal circumstances (if such circumstances exist) so that we can see where the problems might be when things aren't that normal. As we find out more about how our brains function, we will see how the dyspraxic child is the victim of things over which they have no control at all. We will see how the origins of the condition lie at the earliest stages of brain tissue development in the womb.

An overview

A simple overview is that the brain is made up of neurons which are connected by nerve fibres, or axons, to their various destinations in the body. They are arranged in lobes. There are four lobes in each of two hemispheres – the frontal, parietal, temporal and occipital lobes. There is a sharp division of labour within the brain so that different functions of the body are controlled by different parts of the brain.

Messages and information travel along nerve fibres by way of the spinal cord, for example. The huge volume of incoming information from the senses – touch, taste, sight, smell, hearing, movement, balance, warmth, language, experience, sense of self – is organized and stored in the brain, to be retrieved for use as it is needed. All the information needs to be processed, sorted and stored properly, so that it can be pulled out quickly when it is required. If you imagine the brain as a complicated filing cabinet, then you will understand that the brain requires a highly efficient filing clerk if it is to function successfully.

This is an extremely simple picture of what goes on inside your head. The reality is staggeringly more complex but what we have here is probably enough to be going on with.

Disruption

When you consider how complex the brain is, it is not a surprise that a minor disruption can have far-reaching and unpredictable consequences. This disruption, which can cause not only dyspraxia but also other things, can happen as the brain develops in the womb, though no causes for such problems have yet been convincingly identified. It just happens. A weakness, an unexpected connection or the absence of a connection between neurons can be established at any time. If it does happen, then suddenly you are different. The possibility for re-wiring doesn't exist.

Developmental stages

You will know that the pre-birth growth of a baby goes through clearly defined developmental stages. From the moment of conception the fertilized egg divides and multiplies. But some cells will separate from the rest and continue to multiply at their own increased rate to become the nerve cells (neurons) of the brain.

After six months' gestation, the neurons, with their axons, have been produced and subsequently no further new neurons are grown. Furthermore, they do not regenerate. This is an important point. A neuron that is damaged or dies, or does not complete its growth and thus reach its destination, will not be replaced or renewed, unlike cells in other parts of the body. So, if a cell or group of cells fails to complete its growth and thus fails to reach its destination, future sensory information from that area will be impaired. A route will not be established; a connection will not be formed; it won't work as it should. This idea of connections not quite reaching the right destination is a crucial point in understanding dyspraxia.

This system failure can happen in any part of the brain, whether that part deals with movement, speech, emotion. Hence the wide-ranging nature of dyspraxia. So if you are looking for a simple explanation of the origins of the condition, then it is here: dodgy wiring.

A development that does continue, and indeed does so until old age, is that of the individual cells. They grow dendrites. These are branches that reach out and form connections within the brain. There are billions of neurons in every brain, each with many connections with other cells. The infinite number of such combinations is what makes every brain unique. Neurons are connected within your brain that are not connected in the same way in mine. Or in Shakespeare's. Or in Mozart's. Or in Hitler's. This is why there is an infinite variety among us all.

For correct operation, these neurons have to develop in sufficient numbers in the right areas of the brain and they must extend to the correct destination. This has to be achieved by the appropriate developmental stage or it will never occur at all.

There are two kinds of neurons – those carrying messages to the brain (sensory) and those carrying messages from the brain (motor). The implications of inadequate development in either direction are obvious. Any message within the brain can be disrupted.

After six months' gestation, the axons begin to develop an insulating fatty sheath called myelin. This is important because it allows messages to be carried efficiently along the axons. The best analogy is that it functions rather like the insulation around an electric wire. Without it the messages or impulses would fly around everywhere. The myelin makes sure that the messages are concentrated, controlled and heading for the correct destination. It takes time for this protective sheath to be completed. It is in place by around three months of age; babies younger than that will make random reactive movements, without purposeful intent. After myelination, movements will slowly become more deliberate, with purpose and intention. The eyes may become more focused, and the baby may recognize or touch a face and smile. The development of the myelin sheath explains why young children tend to be clumsy and also why some professionals are reluctant to give an early diagnosis of dyspraxia. We all go through a stage when we exhibit some of the symptoms, but it is a stage that most of us leave behind as our brains mature.

The successful creation of such secure message paths is a vital part of our development. It is interesting to note that multiple sclerosis is a direct result of a partial breakdown of the myelin sheath and, as a result, message-carrying capacity.

Dendrites are the connecting branches between nerve cells, and synapses are minute gaps across which impulses pass inside the brain. These continue to increase throughout a lifetime. Their development is stimulated by the demands of the environment, by relationships, experience, and as learning takes place. The very act of reading this book causes changes to take place inside parts of your brain. Through my words I can cause new connections to be established. It is a huge responsibility.

Our own unique view of the world

As we have said, every brain is different, with a unique set of connections. These are the things that make all of us so very different and which give rise to our personal contribution to the world around us. No one sees the world in exactly the same way. This is the basis for humour. A unique and surprising connection is made between thoughts or events. It is something that hasn't occurred to us before. But someone else has seen it. Why didn't we? We didn't see it because our brains were busy seeing other things.

Why is one person good at languages while their sister can barely string two words together? How can twin brothers both become international football players but with different levels of skill? It is because our brains are organs of staggering complexity with an infinite set of possible connections within them. In some people certain connections are securely established. In others they are not. So which one is normal?

Think for a moment . . .

Think about the different skills and talents displayed by people you know.

Would it be possible for others to acquire these things to the same level simply through observation?

In the end, how do you define what a normal brain is like? I believe you can examine the details of conditions like dyspraxia, dyslexia, autism, Asperger's with an alarming sense of familiarity. We all seem to carry elements of them within ourselves, to varying degrees, even Tourette's on a particularly bad Monday. It is all about degree. In most of us they are small parts of our individuality. They don't take over. In some the symptoms are more prominent. It is our individual brain connections that make each of us very different people. They are truly staggering organs that have evolved to the extent that they can design complex computers which in turn perform a range of intricate functions, including designing computers themselves, but none of them can match the wonder of the human brain.

Our brains can process a huge amount of information in an individual way. They are involved in a huge amount of traffic every day and if messages, like trains, can't get through straight away, then they have to be re-routed. Hence delays and disruption when there are neurological leaves on the line.

Indeed, the idea of a railway network is perhaps a good way of presenting the idea of dyspraxia and may prove a useful comparison to share with a dyspraxic child who is anxiously trying to understand what is happening to them.

There are all these messages whizzing round the brain on special tracks and sometimes there is something blocking the line. So the message goes the long way round. It needs to find a different way into the station.

Perhaps you can come up with something better. Please try. It shouldn't be too hard.

Development activity 3: Vocabulary

Make a list of the technical words you have encountered in this section.

Then add their definitions.

This could prove to be an important reference list for you, not only with reference to dyspraxia but also for other conditions.

Praxis

The term 'dyspraxia' comes from the Greek word *praxis*, which means doing, acting, deed or practice. Praxis is a central thing about us as beings. It links what goes on in our heads with what we actually do. It enables us to function in our world by linking the brain and behaviour. So we can dress, eat with cutlery, write, catch a ball, swim. These might not be instinctive actions. They are things that we plan to do. We don't make a cup of tea at an instinctive level. We think through a series of actions. Most animals don't have a great deal of praxis. It is one of the essential things that make us what we are. It makes us human beings. We have an idea and we can think through a series of actions to make it happen. It might be a familiar idea or a completely new one. But through it we change the world around us.

How our brains tell us what to do

Praxis develops as connections are refined in the brain. As we grow, we carry out actions of increasingly better quality, allowing us to do things that are more complicated. Look at a baby. It begins by making largely uncontrolled movements, waving arms and legs around without much of a purpose. Soon these actions are controlled by the will and carried out with premeditated purpose – to touch a rattle, to look at mother. This involves some motor planning, some praxis. These actions are not random or accidental. The child is recalling previous actions and repeating them, modelling what it does now on what it successfully achieved before. Actions soon become more complicated as the brain acquires more retrievable memory of movement sequences. It can access these patterns with increasing success and efficiency because it has stored this information and knows how to find it. When it happens properly, the brain's filing clerk can bask in the warm glow of success, like an informed teaching assistant.

Learning to talk, for example, requires us to organize a specific combination of muscles to produce the right controlled collection of sounds in the right sequence at the appropriate time to achieve a planned purpose. It is what we do when we talk. Think about it. We have something that we need to express, we form the words, and the muscles arrange themselves in the correct way so that we can make structured sounds that others can recognize.

This is praxis – and this is the source of the problem for dyspraxics. The brain sends out a message but it either never arrives or it staggers into the station after the moment has gone. There is no super-fast, multi-lane highway. Just a narrow country track with grass growing in the middle and a tractor blocking the road.

Think for a moment . . .

Think about the sort of physical activities you find difficult to master.

Which activities, on the other hand, can you manage with greater success?

How important are these activities that make up your physical success and under-achievements?

Are there other areas where reduced efficiency would have greater impact on your life?

3

Where it all goes wrong

Let's go back to the three processes involved in carrying out an action, because if we look at how an action happens, we can see where it goes wrong for the child with dyspraxia.

Ideation

If a child comes across some wooden blocks for the first time, they must gather as much information about them as possible. What shape are they? How do they feel? How do they behave? Are they stable or mobile? If my own children are anything to go by, they will also need to find out what they taste like as a matter of some urgency. That information has to be collected, arranged and stored. There's never a moment's peace for that filing clerk.

Then, when required, the information can be retrieved and the knowledge of that experience can be used to form the idea of building something with the bricks. The child knows that they are stable and flat and that they sit together happily. They know that they taste of paint. Now, to build something with them, the child needs a plan of action.

Motor planning

This planning happens in the parietal lobe of the brain. When it receives the idea, the planning department has to work out and plan the instruction it has received. Which part of the body should be where, which particular muscles should contract or relax, in what sequence and by how much. It needs to remember the experience that was gathered about these blocks. This will refine the instructions it is about to send out – the weight of the blocks, the size – and determine the sequence in which the muscles are to work. Then it is time to send out the messages for action.

Execution

Muscles can only either contract or relax in response to messages received from the brain telling it what to do, for how long and in what order. Messages then travel back from the muscle to the brain so that the action can be monitored and revised. We all do this all the time. And we do it very quickly.

The complexities of simple things

When you see the process broken down in this way, then it is a wonder anything ever happens at all. Described in this way it seems so complex. The simple act of stirring a cup of tea seems impossible. But consider this. If there were sand at the bottom of the cup, then the muscles in your hand would flash a message back to the planning department and, if they were not out to lunch, they would work out what was going on by comparing this experience with a previous one: 'Something feels wrong. It is not like it was when I stirred before. It is not dissolving like sugar . . .' and so on. Information is flying backwards and forwards all the time as the situation is assessed. It is not long before a conclusion is formed.

The three stages are interdependent and for the success of any action they rely upon the messages travelling on the correct tracks and making the correct connections. If anything interrupts the messages or if the planning department is indeed out to lunch and the brain can't recall doing this action before quickly enough, then the process will be disrupted. And that is what dyspraxia does for you. The delays may be measured in nanoseconds but they are significant enough because the responses and the function are, as a result, noticeably slower than those of the rest of us.

Think for a moment . . .

Think about a simple action you do every day.

Plan out the steps required to achieve the anticipated outcome in precise detail.

See how complex it appears.

The way in which we learn things is an ordered process. Certain skills must be mastered first and then other skills are added on top of them. You learn to count first and only then can you begin to learn how to add and subtract. So any disruption in the learning process for any skill will affect the subsequent mastering of the later skills that depend upon it. So when we consider dyspraxics, it is not that they will never be able to learn things. The reality is that it will take them so much longer to do it, with lots of stops and starts along the way.

For them, in all this complexity of information-gathering and delivery, something is going wrong. The messages are not getting through or are not producing the right results.

Perhaps the information was not collected or transmitted or stored properly. Perhaps it was stored in the wrong place. Perhaps it was taken out and then put back in the wrong place – and we all know how frustrating that can be. That filing clerk has a lot to answer for. Or alternatively, perhaps the planning department didn't send the messages to the correct destination. Perhaps the right nerve fibres are missing or are incomplete.

Whatever is happening, the praxis is failing. So the child may not be able to pick up the bat quickly enough to hit the ball, or they may not be able to work out how to move from chewing to swallowing. This is also why dyspraxia can be such an inconsistent condition. Yesterday the messages were getting through, the information was retrieved and the task completed. They could colour in the clown without straying outside the lines. Today the plan has been lost. The filing system broke down. It was put back in the wrong place. They can't colour in the clown. Of course the file may turn up again tomorrow, but we can't be sure. The child may just have to relearn the skill.

Colouring in is a simple example, but there could be a system malfunction at any location in the brain. Just imagine how complicated things can become if there is a problem in the area that sorts out relationships and emotions. You cannot approach anything with confidence.

Dealing with incoming messages

There is a similar problem here for dyspraxics. Incoming signals from the environment are not switched automatically to the correct place but must search through a mass of dendrites and may use a tangle of pathways to get to a destination instead of selecting the correct one.

This explains why dyspraxic children use lots of unnecessary movement. It is quite possible that messages could be travelling to all four limbs instead of the one or two necessary to complete an action. There is a fundamental lack of precision. It is interesting to note that assessments that ask dyspraxic children to walk on the outside of their feet show them curl their arms in front. There is simply an unnecessary connection that links these two actions within their brains.

There can also be delays in responding to instructions, and poor coordination when different body parts have to be used together or in sequence. Essentially, there is just too much traffic to deal with efficiently. All the information is piled in at one end but it needs to be sorted, and the motor responses required emerge from this jumble rather too slowly. Information overload, pure and simple, and many of us know precisely how unpleasant that can feel. Remember, with a dyspraxic child they might be experiencing those unpleasant and confusing feelings for most of the time. Imagine how that would affect you.

Development activity 4:
Comparisons

In this section I have used a number of different comparisons to show how dyspraxia operates and how it might thus be explained.

Try and establish your own comparison which you can use to help a dyspraxic child understand what is happening to them.

Then think about how you could present this to the learner and what props you might need to illustrate your comparison.

The next stage then is to try it out!

How do you think it went?

4

The dyspraxic child and the teaching assistant

Dyspraxia isn't a sudden fashion. Dyspraxia isn't a new and trendy creation. It is something that appears in all cultures; it isn't something that is peculiar to English-speaking brains. It has been there for as long as the brain has been operating. It is obvious really. The brain is so complex, it can't be a surprise if parts of it are wired up differently. All our brains work differently and they process all our different experiences, seeing insights, forming connections. And each brain does it differently.

Why is one person good at billiards and their brother absolutely useless? Why is handwriting so unique? How did Shakespeare write as he did? Why do some ideas leap into your mind from nowhere?

Our brains process all our different experiences, seeing insights, forming connections. And if one part of the brain isn't talking successfully to another, then things are bound to be unpredictable. This is what life is about. We are individual human beings, we are not termites. We need to value the different brains we have, because of the different insights that they bring. Difference isn't a threat; it is a cause for celebration. But there is no doubt that the dyspraxic brain brings with it its own challenges. Which is why children with dyspraxia need sympathy and support.

Being with a dyspraxic child

Never forget that dyspraxia is a disability. Even if it is hidden from view, it is still a real disability and it doesn't require a great deal of digging to uncover the evidence of the effects it has. But in a busy school, if the learner is bright and well behaved, then their problems might be minimized or even overlooked. Those dyspraxic learners with whom you are working will be matched by others who have no support because their condition remains unrecognized.

If they learn to disguise their physical shortcomings by avoiding difficult situations, by being ill during PE lessons, by developing a deserved reputation for impenetrable hand-writing, they might get away with it. But the emotional issues will always be lurking in the background, to be eventually exposed by the cruel assaults on their self-esteem that daily life in school can mount.

They may find it difficult to build successful relationships within their own peer group. They might avoid group activities, preferring solitary play, and their lack of social skills means others can't accept them. They can be perceived as odd because their thought processes are different, making their conversation strained.

Make no mistake about it, being with dyspraxic children can be hard work. The connections that others see as a conversation develops are not recognized and what they say can seem irrelevant. They can seem out of sync with everyone else, a couple of paces behind. Their behaviour can seem immature.

A dyspraxic is often a boy who isn't very good at the things a boy is supposed to be good at. He will be poor at sport. Even simple things like kicking and throwing can be challenging. Because of these experiences, his self-esteem will be a fragile thing indeed. A cross word or a family spat and he can be in pieces, sobbing on the bedroom floor. The feeling that he might have disappointed his parents or teachers leads to heart-wrenching and disproportionate despair.

Problems with language

There is sometimes one thing that exposes a dyspraxic learner to others, and that is a problem with speech and the processes that underpin it. For a start, dyspraxia can affect the production of sounds because it can affect those muscles that control speech. The organization of language in the brain may be affected. So, poor sequencing skills may affect the order of letters in words or the order of words within a sentence. A dyspraxic child could have difficulty in identifying the right sounds. Imitating sounds, whistling, blowing balloons could all be impossible. It is not a surprise that a diagnosis of dyspraxia is often made by speech therapists.

Naturally enough, if a child can't relate a letter or combination of letters to the sound it produces, they will struggle to grasp spelling patterns. Making the sounds themselves calls upon organization and coordination to move the muscles sufficiently in the correct sequence. If you can't manage this effectively, what sort of sounds are you going to produce? What will your reputation become in such circumstances? And you will then be considered, at best, as a follower, if you are not rejected completely.

Words are often troublesome. If the learner cannot find the right words quickly enough in their heads, then their ability to tell a story or to recount an event may become confused or lengthy. If they cannot organize their thoughts, they will struggle to establish an order. So there could be lots of repetition, hesitations, false starts. It will require a great deal of effort. What I see, as the father of a very intelligent dyspraxic boy, is that his brain moves so much faster than his sounds. So he has to stop what he is saying in order to allow the production of sounds to catch up. I know that if we could invent telepathy, he would be fine. But others draw disparaging conclusions from conversation that often lacks a natural flow. It is easy to feel that such a brain is trapped. There are other dyspraxic children for whom the spoken word has fewer problems. Their difficulties emerge in writing. When so much assessment requires competent writing, imagine how teachers might respond. Your job must be to intervene on their behalf.

Sensitive skin

In the sensory area there could be symptoms and these will reveal themselves at an early stage. The child might have a poor sense of touch – or even an overdeveloped one, which could mean that certain textures are very difficult to deal with. Some dyspraxic children find that having their hair brushed or cut is very uncomfortable. They can react strongly to having their nails cut. For them, the sensations are felt more intensely than normal. Some children cry because it hurts so much. The labels on clothes have been known to cause extreme irritation. Such extreme sensitivity makes the world a harsh and a cruel place, particularly when others cannot understand it and trivialize such difficulties.

There are other dyspraxic children can't bear to be touched at all. Even brushing lightly against them can cause an over-reaction. They might lash out – to the surprise of those around them. This unexpected behaviour marks them out as unusual and unpredictable.

It might be that they cannot endure holding hands in a circle. Other children naturally feel rejected since they can't understand the reasons for such a refusal and take it personally. Slowly the dyspraxic child becomes someone to be avoided. So, while taking hands in a circle or in a line may sound like a simple instruction, to a dyspraxic child, it can be truly miserable and painful. What are they to do: follow the instruction and be in pain, or ignore it and be in trouble? And, of course, this is something that no one else can ever understand. They could also have problems in blocking out unwanted sounds in order to concentrate on a specific one. It must be like trying to concentrate on a poetry reading in the middle of a disco.

This might provide a useful way of trying to understand what dyspraxic children face in their day-to-day lives. They are swamped by a flood of information that overwhelms them before they can process it. They can't cut out visual and/or auditory 'distractors' from the environment around them. While most of us learn to focus on important signals, those affected by dyspraxia can't ignore other distractors. They cannot filter. So when they need to stop what they are doing and look elsewhere, or when they constantly hear other sounds instead of the teacher, their concentration goes. It can be hard to restore.

Consequently, some noise-sensitive children will give up the struggle to hear clearly and disappear into their own imaginary world. Then, of course, they can be accused of lacking concentration, which is unfair, because the ordinary world as we experience it shouts them down. Where else can they go? The world inside their heads is so much easier.

School can become such a struggle. They are obliged to focus on something that is slipping through their fingers and, at the same time, constantly rebuild a series of individual actions to achieve a particular purpose, working so much harder than the rest of us to do so. It is no wonder that they can be exhausted when they come home from school. Everything they do needs a strained and frustrating level of concentration. Odd. Naughty. Anti-social. Suddenly they have a label. None of this helps a dyspraxic child to build bridges with others in their class. It can drive them into isolation.

Development activity 5:
Sensitivity

Assess this section about physical sensitivities.

In which parts of the curriculum and at which parts of the day will such difficulties become most acute?

Knowing where things are

It will not be a surprise to learn that buttons and, especially, shoelaces can be impossible for a dyspraxic child because of an inability to judge where body parts like fingers are at a particular moment. This is significant. A dyspraxic child will have no sense of placement. If they want to climb onto a chair, they will look to check where the supporting foot is in relation to the chair – they won't be able to sense its position. This is because their proprioceptors, or nerve endings in the muscles and skin, are not relaying information as they should. Quite simply, they don't feel that they can rely upon their body. Parts of it are never where they think they should be.

As a result, they find it really difficult to orientate themselves in space with any efficiency. They thump around. They misjudge distances. Their positional sense is flawed. They are clumsy, untidy, ungainly. It is no wonder that an early term for dyspraxia was 'clumsy child syndrome'.

That child who is always sharpening their pencil because they press on it too hard could have dyspraxia. The end of the pencil and the paper are never quite where they thought they were.

Lots of actions are affected. Sitting down without looking involves a judgment of where the body is in relation to the chair and this, in turn, gives you additional information. It tells you how much strength or release of strength is required to carry out the movement properly. A child lifting a cup needs to know where and when to curl their fingers round the handle and how much strength to use so that the liquid does not spill.

Those, like yourself, with efficient proprioceptors will manage these things automatically. You don't often spill that cup of coffee and you certainly don't think about it every step of the way. In fact, you can pick up the cup and sit down on that chair behind you at the same time. What talent. A dyspraxic child will hold a cup against themselves for extra support and have to look closely at the process at every stage to make sure that neither their body nor the cup betrays them. And in their world the chair they are aiming to sit on is never where they thought it was.

When I run and kick a ball, or when I am trying to hang a piece of wallpaper, I don't have to work out every individual movement separately. The action comes as a package and I can concentrate on it without having to worry about the rest of my senses being overwhelmed. I can call upon the collection of remembered actions to perform the task and continue a conversation or listen to the radio at the same time. It happens all the time – writing, washing, chopping carrots. There are things that we do every day, that we take for granted, that a dyspraxic child could find tremendously difficult – like stepping on and off an escalator. They can't move fluidly because the messages aren't getting there efficiently. If you are a dyspraxic, then there is a thick veil between you and your place in the world.

Think for a moment . . .

Think about how clumsiness can influence the ways others think about an individual.

Just think of the frustrations of being able to see instantly what you need to do but having always to persuade your muscles to catch up. A top-class cricketer has instant coordination between eye and hand. When you watch them in full flow, their anticipation and reactions appear almost magical. By the time the dyspraxic has worked anything out, it is too late. It must feel as if you are in slow motion and the world is whizzing around you at double speed and swamping you before you are ready. I would suspect that many of us feel like this at times. The dyspraxic learner feels like this all the time.

Frustrations

Sometimes dyspraxic children can be physically aggressive, lashing out in frustration at family and friends and showing a complete inability to explain why they have acted as they have.

You can imagine that living with a dyspraxic can be very trying. Their frustrations can take a number of forms. They demand the sort of patience that comes from knowledge and understanding. Sometimes parents haven't got all the information they need. A teaching assistant could be just the person to help them acquire it.

Helping families

Families will need help in dealing with the misunderstandings of the ill-informed who will label their child as lazy or difficult.

- They will need reassurance and strategies.
- They will need to know that someone is interested and that they can put the difficulties they are facing as a family into a context.
- They will need to know that someone cares and recognizes the qualities of their child.
- In short, they might need an advocate.

Think for a moment . . .

Think of all the teachers who work in your school, who do you think is most sympathetic towards learners with dyspraxia?

Who is the most unsympathetic?

What reasons do you have for these opinions?

Why do you think these teachers behave in this way?

Family is very important to the dyspraxic child. It should provide security and happiness, a haven from a complex and confusing world. Sadly this isn't always the case – and difficulties can be magnified hugely if that security disappears with the collapse of a family. In these circumstances you might become more important than you ever intended to be.

A dyspraxic child can certainly create tensions within a family unit because they are so demanding. They will need extra attention and their parents can expect to act as intermediaries between them and the outside world in a more sustained way than they will with their other children. Other family members – as well as the child themselves – will need to understand the full implications of the condition. If it affects one child, then the knock-on effects will impact on all family members. It's inevitable. But knowledge could defuse jealousy.

A dyspraxic child might, in fact, be happiest when at home. It is a predictable environment, safe and controlled. This is quite a contrast with the attitude of many other teenagers, who try to distance themselves from their parents. It is something else that marks out dyspraxics as different.

What is quite possible is that because the real world is so frustrating and depressing, the dyspraxic child will retreat from it. They might inhabit a fantasy world or a world of endless plans. What will happen in the future, what they will do, what they will become. This focus on the future as a means of escape does not mean that they are ever likely to achieve these things. Such a focus brings with it no practicalities or strategies to achieve goals or to realize plans. It is an imaginary world, peopled by imaginary friends, full of plans and schemes, full of easy successes.

At examination time particularly, it might be necessary to encourage them to focus upon the present. It is achievement now that could make their future attainable. Plans made need to be turned into reality, and the only way that will happen is through organization and planning – and, as we've noted, the dyspraxic child will need help to do this. Of course, in this they are no different from many of their peers. But with the dyspraxic it co-exists with so many other symptoms and difficulties.

Being different

The emotional immaturity that comes with dyspraxia can extend childhood well into the teenage years. A dyspraxic child gives you unconditional love and reliance. They rely entirely upon home. This certainly suits some parents who may not want their children to fly the nest. Others will be forever worried about the sort of independent future their child will be able to create for themselves.

Dyspraxic children are emotionally fragile and can be easily hurt. A harsh or unkind word expressed in the heat of the moment can have a disproportionate effect.

Their interest and knowledge can be unexpected and astonishing. They can become almost obsessive about a topic or issue to the extent that it can dominate their lives. Yet they cannot always show sufficient concentration to achieve in a conventional sense in school.

All this is a genuine frustration for parents, for such developmental problems can seem to be a punishment for having a high IQ. They might have to work extremely hard to convince others that their child has talents and abilities, once the fog that surrounds them has been penetrated.

A dyspraxic child is different, and the condition affects every facet of the learner's life. It goes way beyond inabilities with words or pens or physical movement. It might begin with movement but it will impact most profoundly on communication, and social and emotional development. It is in these areas that the parents will need to confront major problems and fears. It is part of your role as an informed adult to offer them reassurance, knowledge, sympathy and solutions. One of the things that is so difficult for parents is that there are no physical attributes that distinguish their dyspraxic child from anyone else. They do not carry a label that allows strangers to stare at them. They look like everyone else. Yet they are truly different.

Development activity 6: Sensitivity

Consider the comments here about families.

What do you think would be the major difficulties facing a family with a dyspraxic child?

Share your thoughts with a colleague.

I am absolutely convinced that if you think back to your own schooldays you will remember an odd boy who didn't quite fit in and who perhaps was laughed at or picked on. Perhaps you knew someone who took his bag away and hid it. But his bag was not his only burden. He was probably carrying dyspraxia around with him too.

Think for a moment . . .

Think about your own schooldays. Can you remember anyone who may, in retrospect, have displayed the symptoms of a dyspraxic learner?

How did you regard them?

How did you respond to them?

How were they treated?

Do you know what happened to them in later life?

As a professional, it isn't long before you come to share a dyspraxic child's frustration. You know how intelligent they are, the talents that they have. You have worked closely with them.

Yet everything has to be accomplished through grey, obscuring wisps of fog. They can see what they want to do. But it is too slippery. It is almost within their grasp – but not quite there. Their intelligence makes them acutely aware of the implications of their condition. They know that they can't do things that others can. Their world-view can become dominated by a sense of inadequacy. You need to make sure that they keep on trying.

Patience and simplicity

You need to keep in mind this idea of an unconventionally wired brain. The information or the knowledge of how to carry out a specific action is in there somewhere. It has just been stored in the wrong drawer. And you will never find your socks if you put them in your pants drawer. Imagine how this would over-complicate your morning if your alarm clock didn't go off and you are already late for work.

Perhaps this silly analogy can point us towards something sensible. You might be able to stop putting your socks in the wrong drawer if it is clearly labelled. That is what dyspraxic children sometimes need. A bit of basic organization. Simple solutions. They might not be able to fasten shoelaces but does that matter? Buy elastic-sided shoes or trainers. Why was Velcro invented? They will need other people around them to help them find such solutions. That's what you do with dyspraxia. You work with it. You work around it.

We can all become hung up on the causes. We can explore brain function and development and very interesting it is too. It is the only way to achieve a full and detailed understanding of dyspraxia. But the causes will still remain unclear. What teachers need to do is to deal with the means by which we intend to manage the condition in the classroom, so that we can access the potential of each child and support the parents who are trying to manage a difficult domestic situation.

Being a teaching assistant

In case you needed reminding, working with children, in whatever capacity, is more than just a job. Teachers and teaching assistants have the opportunity, through their understanding and sympathy, to influence lives in radical ways. So look at your title. You are not a teacher's assistant, one who is employed to clean the white board. You are a teaching assistant and your job is to make sure that teaching and learning are effective. You don't make the tea; you change lives. This is why you chose the job and this is why you keep on doing it. Never regard yourself as an unimportant cog in the wheel. Dyspraxics and their families need the skills and understanding you can offer. There is no progress without you.

The skills and qualities you will need

First and foremost you will need **patience**. Dealing with dyspraxic learners and their sometimes sceptical teachers isn't easy. There are no overnight solutions. Small steps, tiny triumphs, but they go together eventually to make something bigger and ultimately significant.

You will need to show unswerving **commitment** to all the learners you have assigned to you, even the ones you don't like. It is a professional job and requires a professional attitude. You are in this for the long haul.

You must have **belief**. You must believe that you are doing an important job. You may not see instant results but you need to realize that in the long term you will have an impact. It might be you who gives a learner the support at a crucial time that later in their life keeps them out of prison. You will never be able to prove that connection, but you must always believe that what you are doing truly matters.

You must show **imagination**. Look for interesting new ways to deal with problems. Just because something worked once with one learner is no guarantee that it will work again. In this way, you will not stagnate but instead keep your brain alive.

A teaching assistant will need to display **courage**. There will be those who say that dyspraxia isn't a real condition. You will need to defend that particular corner and also stand up for the dyspraxic learner among their peers if necessary.

You must show a willingness to involve yourself in all aspects of the dyspraxic's education, even in those areas where you feel less confident, like PE for example.

Involvement will set an excellent example to the learner themselves and perhaps encourage them to get more involved too. You are a full part of the school.

Be **analytical**. You will need to look at what is happening around you in the school and assess how this is impacting on dyspraxic learners. Then you will need to think about how you can make things more successful.

Organization at a personal level is important. Apart from the positive benefits it brings to all of us in our professional lives, you really need to set a good example. If you are offering advice to others on the importance of organization, then you need to show this quality yourself. So always be punctual; always have a pen; always know what is going on.

Resilience is a key quality. Remain convinced about what you are doing even when the dyspraxic you are investing so much time and energy in is rejecting what you have to offer. There might, as you can see, be reasons for this. So you just have to keep going back for more.

Above all, you will need to show a desire to **learn**. This is definitely what the best teachers do. They learn something new every day that they can apply to their job. You should be no different. You need to carry on reading this book and then think carefully about what you have read. You should apply what you have read to real-life dyspraxic learners. And then you will be doing the job that you signed up for.

Think for a moment . . .

Think about how you are going to extend your understanding further.

Is there anyone you should talk to?

Are there any other books you should read?

Have you done an internet search about 'dyspraxia'?

5

What are the signs?

This is the first, and the greatest, of all the problems associated with dyspraxia: it doesn't have a common set of symptoms. Scarlet fever or mumps are both pretty easy to diagnose, since everyone suffers in largely the same way. With dyspraxia, each person is affected in different ways and to different degrees.

In the majority of cases, parents are the first to notice it. They will get anxious because developmental stages may not be reached or negotiated. The child may be late in learning to sit, stand, or walk. Even doting grandparents will notice. When it comes to crawling, some dyspraxic children never manage it at all. If this particular inability is noted, it can represent a defining moment.

Crawling and eating

There are good reasons why the dyspraxic brain may not allow its host (or child, as we like to call it) to crawl, because the required skills of coordination, sequential movement and balance are just too difficult to organize. It involves balancing in a safe prone position, stretching out in different directions and coordinating all four limbs to achieve a predetermined purpose. It sounds much more difficult than it is for most of us.

Crawling is significant because an inability to crawl affects the acquisition of other skills, such as throwing, catching and climbing. These also require balance and timing and spatial orientation. Never dismiss the importance of crawling, for there are those who suggest that this early lack of sequencing practice inhibits reading, pointing out that many dyslexic children never learn to crawl either. Finding out that a child had difficulty crawling could be a highly significant piece of evidence. Naturally, the most reliable source of such information is the parents themselves. So never dismiss as unimportant what they have to tell you.

Other expected skills may not be mastered. My own son experienced considerable feeding difficulties. As a young child he was not able to coordinate swallowing efficiently. Other children may be messy eaters who spill things all the time or are especially inefficient in dressing themselves. Shoelaces could prove to be an impenetrable mystery and indeed remain so, until the dyspraxic brain comes to the conclusion that it must allow its host to wear elastic-sided shoes. Other routine tasks of daily life could prove impossible. If you try slicing an onion while wearing mittens you might get some idea of what it can be like, though I would not recommend it.

Shame

The dyspraxic child learns to live with shame because of their complete inability to carry out everyday tasks that the rest of the population appear to do instinctively. If anything was ever likely to make you feel like a freak, it is this.

Symptoms

Here are some other symptoms. Remember, this is not an exhaustive list. To have these symptoms does not make you dyspraxic, but have an accumulation of them and you could well be a contender.

We can all exhibit the first one, and probably do, as the others who share our lives will testify, and many of us have the second one. But go down the list and see how they begin to represent a considerable weight that you would prefer not to carry with you as you go about your daily business. Then give thanks for the fact that you don't have to, and realize that for many dyspraxics, these are the veil through which they see the world. Everything for them becomes blurred and muddy.

- Irritability and poor sleep patterns
- Poor writing and drawing ability
- Inability to stay still
- Difficulty in going up and down hills
- A lack of rhythm
- Short attention span
- Difficulty in carrying out instructions
- Frequently falling and bumping into things
- Poor posture and fatigue
- Too trusting, with little sense of danger

Why?

There is no reason why anyone should get dyspraxia. There is a random cruelty about it. It is not a result of eating too much chocolate during pregnancy. It is not a deformity. It does not show up under neurological examination. It is not the consequence of some sort of mistake or mistreatment.

All that can be said is that there may be an inherited tendency that predisposes members of a family to this and to other related conditions. If there is a history of dyspraxia on the mother's side there is a 1 in 3 chance of it being passed on. If it is on the father's side, then the likelihood is almost 2 in 3. But not all children with dyspraxia enjoy such family traditions and other factors have been implicated. There may have been a momentary problem – an illness, a lack of oxygen at a crucial stage of foetal development or at birth that caused damage. Maternal stress during pregnancy has been implicated. Or it could simply be that particular connections between cells are faulty. The fact that it can co-exist with other disorders like dyslexia or Attention Deficit Disorder means that precise diagnosis can be difficult, since all the symptoms intermingle.

The dyspraxic's inability to plan and sequence thought and to predict outcomes is a symptom of a problem deep inside the brain. This is the predictable answer to the question about where it comes from. But the real answer is that it is nothing much more than a roll of the dice.

Will I always be safe?

It is possible to suffer from acquired dyspraxia, which occurs after damage to the brain. It could be the result of a stroke, an accident or a medical disaster. This usually happens to older people and the difference is that they have a memory of praxis that they will need to restore. The machine might have crashed but the information is in there somewhere. You can reboot. You can rescue.

Children with developmental dyspraxia don't have this lost or damaged memory to recover. For them the brain is, literally, immature.

Undiagnosed dyspraxia

Wherever you work within the education system, you might well come across a learner with undiagnosed dyspraxia. Just because there is no record of a learner having the condition, it doesn't mean that they haven't. There are always those who slip through the net, for whatever reason. This is absolutely true and one of the strange coincidences that features in all our lives. When I was writing this section we had a parent's consultation evening in school and I discovered a student aged 16 who was undeniably a undiagnosed dyspraxic. I talked to the parents and I knew. It was obvious. Why had no one in my school seen this before?

So when you have done your research into the condition, trust your judgements and tell someone should you have similar suspicions, and of course present the evidence that you have.

It is most likely, of course, that a teaching assistant will have been involved in the early identification of dyspraxia if they are working with younger learners. There are signs that can be very significant, but the advice here about identification can be appropriate at any stage.

An observant teaching assistant will see a learner and concerns may start to form. They will begin to form a picture. They will slowly accumulate evidence.

Watch out for these signs

You should register concerns when you see a child

- who is less inclined to participate in play, particularly physical games
- who is perhaps less active than the others around them
- who avoids physically challenging situations
- who is more passive and seems more anxious.

The learner's reputation will be established as that of an outsider, slightly beyond the fringe of interaction and group activity. They might want to be part of the crowd but don't seem able to be fully accepted. If you are concerned by the appearance of one symptom then look to see if any others are there.

The process of isolation may either be started or fully established. The dyspraxic child will learn very quickly that there are things they find harder to do than others and even at this young age they will not want to be different from their friends. But they have little choice.

Some dyspraxic learners are hypersensitive to certain stimuli. They might have an aversion to bright lights or loud noises. You can notice this on occasions like Bonfire Night or at discos or at Christmas time. Such an aversion could become discernible if the child is involved in a play or a performance. They could be very uncomfortable under bright lights.

There could be an over-sensitivity to certain textures like the labels on clothes or to wool. Some dyspraxics find that combing their hair is extremely uncomfortable, indeed painful, though in itself it is not conclusive evidence, it may be merely an example of the standard slovenliness of some children.

They may become less articulate when excited or upset. Long stories or explanations can't be sustained and there might be constant repetitions of statements and questions as the child fights to maintain concentration and fix information in their head.

And from many of these issues there is no escape.

What is most frustrating is the inconsistency that comes with dyspraxia. What you know today you may not know tomorrow. The plan needed to perform a task could disappear suddenly, just when you thought it wasn't a problem any more.

Development activity 7:
Review

Review what you have read so far.

What do you now know about dyspraxia that you didn't know before?

Make four lists of bullet points that

a)   outline the causes of dyspraxia;

b)   identify some of the symptoms;

c)   outline the characteristics of the dyspraxic child;

d)   identify the contribution that a teaching assistant could make.

Think for a moment . . .

If these figures are right, then do you think that the other people where you work are aware of the incidence of the dyspraxia?

If not, then why do you think this is so?

Who gets it?

In simple terms, the condition affects up to 4 per cent of the population but at least 70 per cent of those affected are male. Sufferers are generally of average or above-average intelligence. The numbers are significant. They mean that teachers can assume that there is probably at least one child with the condition in every class.

Teaching assistants can be confident that dyspraxia is something that they will have to deal with quite regularly during their work. I have no doubt at all that those of you who have been working as teaching assistants for any length of time will be able to relate the symptoms to children that you already know. This is why dyspraxia is not something that can be easily dismissed. Naturally, in specialist provision the incidence of dyspraxia could well be over 50 per cent.

What do you see around you?

You need to remember that only those children where the disorder seriously impairs learning or development are ever properly diagnosed. There are many others whose dyspraxia is not recognized and who instead are given other labels – like thick or slow or clumsy. If you start thinking of difficult children in classes that you have met, you might be able to see some of the symptoms of dyspraxia in the behaviour they displayed. Or think about children who find it very hard to mix with others around them. Think about those children who have absolutely no coordination at all, who seem to be a complete disaster in PE lessons. Their mild form of dyspraxia might not be enough to get them diagnosed but it will be enough to make their school life difficult. The more you think about it, the more it explains.

Development activity 8: Review

Make a list of those children you know who you feel might display some of the features of dyspraxia.

Now check their records to see whether they have been diagnosed.

Ask more experienced colleagues whether they share your suspicions.

Monitor the children's behaviour over a period of time to see whether your impressions can be supported.

If appropriate, refer your conclusions with evidence to the SENCO or equivalent.

You will also find that thinking about unpredictable developments within the structure and connections of the brain can also help you understand the way some children behave in lessons and around the school. It is not always their fault. Any poor achievement can then lead to low self-esteem and antisocial behaviour. Why engage with something that only ever reminds you of your failure? Better to reject it altogether.

We have all seen this. Some now believe that three-quarters of children with behavioural difficulties have dyspraxia. Among those in young offenders institutions the incidence is equally high. And if we don't do something about it, then things can only get worse.

Of course, not all dyspraxics become delinquent, but they might indeed become disillusioned with a school system that seems to exclude them and thus seek out other areas of interest. If this happens, then their potential will be lost.

Schools need to do their jobs properly and provide dyspraxic learners with the support that will help them build successful lives. In this way, schools try to shape the future. Because, remember, it is in schools where the future is constructed. As a teaching assistant, you share a responsibility for these things. Never forget that you can influence the shape of that future. There is no more important place to work than school – and you have a crucial role within it. So never underestimate the importance of your job or the influence that you have.

Development activity 9: Review

Think about the following questions and write a brief statement for your line manager in which you outline your own point of view.

Do we have a moral obligation to help learners with dyspraxia?

Why should we act to address some of the consequences of dyspraxia?

Wouldn't it be cheaper just to ignore it and thus save money by employing fewer teaching assistants?

If we cannot cure dyspraxia then wouldn't it be better to ignore it and concentrate on other conditions?

6

Parents and actions

Occupational therapists, physiotherapists, speech therapists, teachers, psychologists, educational psychologists or paediatricians can perform tests. But it is the parents of the child who usually carry out the most effective initial diagnosis. They will know that something is wrong. They may not realize what it is, but they will know that something isn't right. They might not be able to articulate it, but they will know. Professionals have to learn to accept this.

Listen

Parents will have noticed difficulties and developmental surprises, perhaps from very early on in the child's life. The child will appear healthy and alert. Yet they will know that something isn't right.

They will want the best for their child. Why shouldn't they? But if a diagnosis has not yet been made, then they may acquire a reputation as fussy parents. In a busy school, their concerns about their child might not yet have featured on the radar. This could certainly affect the way that they are viewed by a school. Professionals should always ask themselves why parents have concerns. Are they legitimate? Are they justified? You need to listen to parents' observations because they know far more about their own child than anyone else. Never dismiss them out of hand.

It could have been a very frustrating time for parents, trying to convince a doctor that something is wrong. It is not unknown for parents to be seen as troublesome because they keep asking questions. They might need someone to take their concerns seriously and to listen. It is a very important time, for it might be when the first interventions and strategies begin. Parents might need you to reassure them that their child's problem with the labels on clothes is neither too alarming nor unique.

Working with parents

Parents will want to know the answers to many questions and they will also want to find out what they can do to make things better for the child that they love.

You should be able to offer them some understanding of the condition, perhaps putting it in terms that they can understand. They might listen more closely to you since you are probably not so intimidating as a teacher. And, of course, in these circumstances you need to remain as positive as possible. They don't need gloom and doom; they can probably provide this for themselves. Tell them that they are not alone and that there are things they can do. These things won't cure it, but they will help to manage the dyspraxia and over time lead to some improvement.

An emphasis upon routine and careful planning at home will be very valuable. A simple series of graded exercises to be carried out either at school or in the home could be proposed. An example could be walking between two lines about a foot apart. This will help coordination and could be part of a game for everyone, not just a child with dyspraxic tendencies. Then they could move on to riding a scooter between the lines. This can take on a more imaginative dimension if this path is imagined as the route to a special place or the route to a reward.

But, of course, the most important question parents will have is whether their child will ever grow out of their dyspraxia. Your professional responsibility is to be honest. They will probably not. What might happen, though, is that over time they will adapt their behaviour to accommodate the difficulties they have. They will learn to live with them and to manage them, if they get the right help. Because what we are looking at here is a severe difficulty, but it is not one that cannot be overcome. How many successful and notable people are there out there who are, in reality, undiagnosed dyspraxics? Look at their handwriting. You decide.

To be honest, I can sympathize with parents entirely. We didn't know what our son's problem was, but we knew he had one. We became very irritated with those who told us that we were merely over-anxious parents. We knew nothing about dyspraxia until an old and wise speech therapist diagnosed it within about 30 seconds of meeting David. Then everything fell into place.

The problem we had was that no one would listen to us when we said that something wasn't quite right. And, surely, no one is in a better place to see these things than the parents. I know you don't need professional qualifications to become one, but being their parent does give you some insight into your own child. Don't ever ignore what parents say. This is a very important point and one we must all remember. Don't ever be part of a conspiracy that dismisses a parent's opinions out of hand. Yes, they may be anxious. They might even appear over-anxious to you, but there might be a very good reason for their anxiety, and who are you to dismiss it?

Listen to them. They might not have a posh job, they might not know very much about the secret workings of the brain, but they know their child. No one knows them better. Some one has to talk to them. Someone has to listen. Often there is no one better placed than you. You probably do not pose the same sense of intimidatory professionalism to some parents as a headteacher in a suit.

Think for a moment . . .

Consider whether the place in which you work has systems in place that will allow parents to express and explore their concerns.

Is there any way in which these systems could be improved?

Now, it is pretty clear that as a teaching assistant you are not going to know about some of the symptoms that the child has displayed. They will have happened at times and in places when you were not around. But you could provide a really useful help to parents who might be struggling to understand what is happening to the child whom they love and who is apparently finding so much of daily life difficult to manage. Ask questions based upon the knowledge you are acquiring.

Parents are often in need of a sympathetic ear, especially if dyspraxia has not yet been diagnosed. So if you have a chance – and if you are working very closely with their particular child, then you must make that chance for yourself – find out more details about the developmental stages that the child has gone through. Find out about their past.

Don't ever think you are going to cure the dyspraxia. Of course you won't. But helping someone find the label that they can stick on it is often vital. Knowing that it has a history and that others have it offers real reassurance. You find out that your child isn't a freak after all. There are books about it, and once it has been identified, you know which part of the shelves to look at. You can search the internet. You can talk to others. Never underestimate how reassuring that can be.

And don't forget that some parents, especially those who don't have very fond memories of school themselves, may feel inhibited or unsettled by teachers. To be honest, I can sympathize entirely, but what is important to them is that you are not a teacher. You are something else, and as a result they might just tell you more than they will ever say to a teacher. You can be a pivotal part of the process that identifies the condition and a crucial element in the strategies that are put in place.

**Development activity 10:
Supporting parents**

Think carefully about what you have read in this section.

Imagine that a distressed parent of a dyspraxic asks you for more information about the condition.

Plan out carefully what you will say, that will both explain the nature of the condition and reassure them about their child.

Then present your summary to a colleague who has only a limited understanding of the condition.

How did they respond to your explanation?

Do they have any advice to offer you?

What should you now do to improve your presentation, before you try it out for real?

So what happens next?

When a child is suspected of having dyspraxia, they should at least be assessed by an educational psychologist with a view to a statement of special educational needs being drawn up. An Individual Education Plan (IEP) will help everyone. You should have an important part to play in this process. It will help teachers to respond to, and plan for, children who are often very talented. It might offer advice to parents about strategies and may suggest possible dietary supplements such as Evening Primrose Oil (EPO) and fish oils which some have found effective. It might well identify the nature and extent of your role.

An Individual Education Plan

This important document will outline all the strategies that the teachers should employ to help the child who holds it. It will provide a framework and offer practical advice. You yourself should be well acquainted with the contents so that you can monitor how specific needs are being met. You should share the contents with any dyspraxic learner you are asked to support so that they are reminded of their side of the bargain that has been struck. It will aid their own understanding.

The IEP will also be essential in guaranteeing for the dyspraxic the extra time in examinations that is their right. Achievement in examinations will have long-lasting consequences.

But, most importantly, both the statement and the subsequent IEP will reassure the child that they are not alone. Their needs and frustrations have been recognized. There are things that will help. It will also reassure parents that their concerns are being taken seriously.

Sometimes it might just feel like another piece of unnecessary paperwork, but it is a process that should have real and lasting benefits. It must never be sidelined or neglected.

Remember: there is a good chance that the child will proceed to further education. In the future, not to do so might be increasingly rare. This means that a statement has consequences for funding and might trigger important support for a family, especially in terms of grants and equipment. This should be explored.

Development activity 11: Documentation

Speak to the SENCO (or equivalent) where you work.

Ask for permission to look at the documentation relating to a particular learner.

What conclusions can you draw from the advice that the documentation contains?

Can you think of any practical solutions to any of the issues that are contained?

Staying informed

What is needed at an institutional level is that the condition is treated with sympathy and from a position of knowledge. There should, ideally, be someone in every school, at every level, who knows something about dyspraxia and can offer some advice. But that someone doesn't have to be a teacher. Why shouldn't it be you?

Dyspraxia is not an isolated condition. There are sufferers in every school, possibly in most classes, and the profile of understanding should be raised. And when you think about the statistics, not only have you already met a child with dyspraxia, but also there is likely to be someone with the condition, in whatever form, in your extended family. How would you want them to be treated if they came to the place where you work?

Development activity 12:
Educational plans

Identify a learner you have observed in the course of your work.

Do not look at their IEP.

Write an IEP for them, based upon what you have seen.

Now compare what you have written with the official version.

What conclusions do you draw?

7

How you can make a difference

I think there are many ways in which you can make a genuine difference. As I said in the previous section, one very important thing you can do is to talk to parents. In fact as an activity, this is about as important as it gets. Don't forget. You are centrally placed in all that goes on in the school, with a unique and un-rivalled impression of what happens in all parts of it. There is no other adult in the school who sits in the range of different lessons that you attend. Not the head teacher, not even an inspector. Not only that, teachers are less inclined to put on a show when you are there, because after a while you become part of the furniture. Is this a good thing or a bad thing? I don't know, but more than anyone else, you know the truth about what goes on, for good and for bad. This means that you can see the lessons from the perspective of a learner in general, and a disadvantaged one in particular.

What exactly is your job?

I've mentioned this before, but let us examine the precise implications of your job title, because it is instructive and very revealing, there for all to see: 'teaching assistant'. The emphasis here is on *teaching*. Not *teacher*. You are employed to assist with teaching, to ensure that teaching, and therefore learning, takes place in a productive atmosphere.

You are not a teacher's assistant. You are not a gopher. If you are sent to go for this or to go for that, then someone needs to have a word. And it will happen. There are many teachers whose one ambition is to find themselves a little servant with excellent tea-making skills. This isn't you.

A teaching assistant must have a more professional and structured role than this. Your focus must be upon the subject matter of the lesson. You are supporting the learner. The teacher is a trained professional interpreting and presenting a scheme of work.

Think for a moment . . .

Make a list of what you consider to be requests which fall within your remit and those which do not.

Ask your colleagues how many similar inappropriate tasks they were offered and how they dealt with them.

What this indictes is that you are an intermediary. You are the filter, you are a channel through which the learning flows. You reshape and reconfigure. You put things into different words. You can reinforce the learning at another place and another time. You might thus in some senses become an additional presenter of this material. In fact, some teachers may regard you warily, since they might see you as an intruder. But there is no way in which you are a teacher. You don't work to a pro-gramme of study. All the decisions about subject matter are not yours. You should have something to offer about how it is presented, but the decisions made by a teacher on the basis of their professional expertise are not yours. You mustn't question them; you must work with them. And at times that can be very hard.

But your role is entirely learner-focused. You have to stand alongside as the subject matter and the learner meet and it is up to you to make sure that their relationship is a happy and fulfilling one.

Work with teachers. You know you want to

You will have a wider perspective because you will see things from across the school as a whole.

> I saw this in art and it worked with Jamie really well. Perhaps it can work here. I'll tell you what, if you let me know what we are doing next lesson then I can put something together.

You are assisting teaching and you are supporting the teacher. You are in this way facilitating learning, you are doing your best to ensure success for both sides.
Or how about this?

> In maths Jamie puts a blob of blue tac on the top of his ruler because it gives something to grip. It might help that girl in the corner. Do you mind if we give it a try.

Think for a moment . . .

Can you think of circumstances where these comments, or something close to them, could be appropriate?

And once you start to offer practical advice and suggestions in this way, then you will quickly be accepted. Teachers are always looking for new ideas and practical solutions; pretty soon you'll be regarded as indispensable. You will be developing and exploiting an expertise which will quickly make you an integral part of the team.

Yours is a fascinating role. You'll find out more about the classroom experience than anyone else. You will be able to sit in the staffroom with a genuinely informed opinion of those people around you. However they try to persuade their colleagues about what happens in their lessons, you will know the truth about what went on and perhaps there will be a time when you keep them on their toes. But, of course, this brings with it a sense of responsibility.

You are a responsible adult, working in the school, with a professional job description. You can't ignore the things that you see. Obviously you can't walk past a fight in the corridor. And you can't ignore a disaster in the classroom. If you are aware of a teacher who is continuously having problems, who is struggling with either the class or the subject matter, then you need to tell someone. No one gains anything if such a situation is allowed to continue, least of all the learners you are supporting. It isn't telling tales. It is doing your job.

If there is a problem, then ignoring it will not make it go away. The only thing that will resolve the difficulty is the act of confronting it, together with others, in a supportive role. In my experience, it is through cooperative and supportive arrangements that issues are resolved. They never go away if they are denied or ignored. So if you see something that really is wrong, if there are situations developing or atmospheres developed that you would not be happy about your own children having to experience, then you must do something about it. It might not be your job to deal with it, but it's your job to tell someone who can. You are not a qualified teacher. But you are a qualified adult and it doesn't require much more than common sense to recognize a disaster. And bad situations rarely get better on their own.

Development activity 13: Referral processes

What are the referral processes that exist in the place where you work?

Who should you speak to if you have concerns about

a) a learner;

b) a teacher or member of staff;

c) a parent or carer;

d) systems and organization?

Are you clear about child protection issues and what procedures you should follow?

Becoming an expert

What I anticipate is that over time you will be regarded as having particular expertise and this will bring with it its own status and rewards. You will be regarded as someone who has a perspective and an awareness, especially if you are dealing with specific learning issues like dyspraxia. From offering advice, you will soon be the person whose opinion is sought out. That relationship with teachers and your intensive support of individuals will be seen as a means of bridging the gap. It will mean that you can be recognized as a person who is task-focused. Your job is to facilitate the learning, to make sure that a learner does not struggle with it, to open windows and doors. However grumpy teachers can sometimes appear, they also want the learning in their classroom to succeed. Their pleasure comes from successful lessons. You can help make that happen.

Your role will develop, I am confident of that. As a result of your sensitive and thoughtful work in the classroom, you will be seen as having specific and practical knowledge. It is quite likely that you will know far more about dyspraxia than many of the teaching staff. So you will be an adviser. You will be able to identify the characteristics of the sort of lesson that will support the learning of dyspraxics wherever they are. Your work will ensure a better experience for dyspraxic learners. That's why they pay you.

Think for a moment . . .

Think about the other professionals in your school. What reasons might they have to regard you as a threat?

Work with another teaching assistant, either within your own institution or in another, and compile a list of difficulties that you believe they may perceive.

What can you do to allay these fears?

Making a judgement about the lessons you are in

Of course, you are not a teacher. You might be very pleased about this, or you might be planning to upgrade your training at some point in order to make that transition. But you will spend an enormous part of your life in the classroom. As we have said, this will give you a very useful perspective. And I am sure that one of the things you will find is that you are able to do your job most effectively in the best lessons. A poor lesson might, in fact, make even greater demands upon you in terms of supporting a learner, but you may not feel that you have been able to do it successfully in an unsatisfactory situation.

So what are the characteristics of a lesson which is successful for learners with dyspraxia?

You will not be surprised to learn that they are generally the characteristics of any successful lesson. First of all, the teacher needs to ensure that instructions are broken down and simplified. This is an important skill which is often overlooked. The best teachers have this ability and yet never recognize that it is there. It is this facility that makes them successful teachers.

Remember, almost everything can be broken down into a staged process with a logical sequence. Any process can be displayed as a flow-chart – writing an essay, making an electrical circuit, making a cup of tea. Again, good teachers are good at this. This is also one of the most important things that a teaching assistant will do when they are working in the classroom. In fact, it is one of the things you will become good at – and all children in a class can benefit from this approach. Certainly, never be surprised if you find yourself helping others around you in the class.

Expectations need to be communicated clearly and concisely. Questions should be asked to ensure everyone knows what to do. A good teacher will offer encouragement and keep reminding the class of the task and the sequence they must follow.

All teachers know that reading, writing and maths all require a great deal of planning and organization. They need to be integrated carefully into the lesson. The very best teachers make this happen seamlessly. The lesson is entertaining and inspiring but leads to other activities. Writing, for example, isn't seen as a chore – and it shouldn't be if the purpose is clear and achievable. In the most successful lessons it is integral and planned. Part of your role is to help to make sure that this planning takes place, for those learners who find the very act of organizing themselves very difficult. You will also need to promote positive attitudes to writing with dyspraxic learners.

We are all surrounded by too many choices that we don't need. So keep choices simple. If the teacher gives the rest of the class a choice between six different essay titles, for example, they will probably direct their students to the ones which they feel they can engage with most successfully. A teaching assistant, too, must consider whether such a wide choice is necessary for their dyspraxic learner. It might, in fact, be much more successful if a teaching assistant were to intervene and discard four of those alternatives immediately. Tell them that they have a choice of two, based upon their knowledge of the learner.

A good teacher ensures that all learners know where they are in the overall shape of the lesson and how much time they have left. They give them clear time checks, making sure there is a clock or a watch visible: 'There are ten minutes to go, so start bringing this section to a close.' This is very important technique to acquire for examinations anyway, and classroom professionals probably won't be there to offer that sort of structure. It is something the learner has to learn.

The best teachers minimize distractions, and a simplified classroom always helps. They keep screens and boards free of unnecessary information as an aid to concentration. This will encourage focus in all learners. This is something that a teaching assistant needs to implement in the learners' work area. A focused desk leads to a focused mind. Reduce graffiti, for it only distracts.

Development activity 14: Judging lessons

Think about the best lessons you have seen where you work.

What characteristics did they have that made them successful?

Where there things within the lesson that could be used in different subject areas?

Now think about the characteristics of the less successful lessons you have seen.

Why wouldn't you want a child of your own to have been part of this experience?

What could have been done to make it better?

Teachers try to achieve all these things because they know that generally they work. They make learning more successful and they make teaching easier and more rewarding. They also know that the bit about the desk is true, but it represents the paradise they know they will never reach.

But you can learn from this. Keeping things simple and focused, avoiding unnecessary distraction, creating a sense of purpose and achievement are exactly the sort of things a teaching assistant is aiming for. And the learner will accept you once they know that you have successful and supportive measures that they understand and can employ.

So watch and learn. Teaching assistants help learners, and watch teachers, which helps you to help learners some more. All you need is a positive and a professional approach to the job. There is more to it than carrying the learner's bag and sharpening their pencils.

**Development activity 15:
Developing materials**

Identify an activity you enjoyed in a subject that you are interested in.

Get a copy of the teaching materials that are used in the classroom.

Adapt them for use by a learner with dyspraxic symptoms.

Show your work to the teacher who originally designed the teaching materials for their comments and show it to your line manager.

8

What you should do

Never forget that there is a structure and a purpose to the role you have been asked to fulfil. There is more to the job than being a nice and friendly person. I don't dispute that these are important qualities. They will help you to be successful in your job and help you to become an accepted part of the place where you work. You will become a popular member of staff. But there must be more to the job than this.

In some schools teaching assistants are known as 'aunties'. In one school near mine they are known as 'The Care Bears'. Very nice too, but there is more to the job than turning up in history and writing stuff down from the board because Jamie or Jordan can't be bothered. You must always be more than the indulgent older brother or sister. Yes, a teaching assistant has to support their identified learners, and that support breeds sympathy and sometimes affection, but that support must also go beyond making them feel comfortable. Learners will need to be challenged and stretched, and sometimes this can be uncomfortable and confrontational. It is called 'tough love', I believe. Remember, it is one thing for a learner to say they can't do something. It is quite another for them to say that they won't do something. You help in one case. You confront in the other.

Focus on learning, not comfort

Your job, as your title indicates, is to facilitate teaching, and by implication learning. Your job is to pander neither to the teacher nor to the learner. You are wedded to learning. It is not that you shouldn't be sympathetic. It is more that you should focus upon the real importance of what you do. Sometimes this emphasis will bring a bit of an edge to your job. But you have to be ready for this. You cannot be all things to all people. If you maintain a focus and are not prepared to abandon your beliefs, then you will have issues to deal with. This is a good thing.

Think for a moment . . .

Think about nicknames. They can be very revealing.

Do the TAs in your institution have an alternative title? If so, then what is it?

What does this tell you about how they are perceived?

Deal with behaviour

If a learner puts their pen down, looks you in the eye and says, despite your best endeavours, that they won't do it, then this is something you have to confront, there and then. It is a challenge that you, and no one else, must be ready to take up. If you don't, or if you refer it to someone else, then your credibility will be shot to pieces. It is you that they have taken on and even if they back down when someone else intervenes, then it probably won't bother them much because they will have triumphed over you. I am afraid to say that it is no more sophisticated than that. It is primitive; it is about power and influence and control; and it is vital.

The learner has to realize that when they cross a line in the sand, then they had better re-assess their position pretty quickly. You have a job to do , and that job is them. It would be nice to think that things such as this will not happen. But in my view they will. You need to be ready for them. A refusal to do something may be born out of frustration or through information overload. You will have shown already a sympathetic willingness to deal with these difficulties, but you must establish clearly and firmly that giving up is not an option. Dyspraxic learners are no different from other learners in this respect. They might be attracted to the easy option, but a central part of your role is to make sure that they don't slip into easy indolence. They will be less inclined to do so if they are aware of their successes. If you have established a warm and supportive relationship, then they will also be inclined to do the things you want because they will want to please you.

Development activity 16: Behaviour

What are the most challenging behaviours you have seen?

How were they managed?

Was this successful?

What did you feel about these incidents?

What else could have been done?

Managing a dyspraxic learner

The following are bits of advice for any adult dealing with a dyspraxic learner. Parent, lecturer, teaching assistant, teacher . . . all require the same qualities and approaches.

- It is important to maintain eye contact when giving instructions to an individual dyspraxic learner. This will help them to concentrate. You will do this. You need to make sure that the teachers understand this too.
- Explain things in a simple, uncomplicated way. Make sure your instructions remain constant and unchanged.

Consistency is the key, because it brings with it a sense of security. It shows the learner that they only have to remember one thing.

- In these circumstances patience is a virtue. Be prepared to repeat yourself calmly and frequently. As a teaching assistant you will do this all the time, but you will need to ensure that the teachers understand the importance of this too. It must always be stressed that the teachers can, and will, learn from well-informed teaching assistants. It is a mutually supportive situation.

- With younger children particularly, it can be helpful to repeat things gently, leading and prompting the memory until previous learning can be recalled. Just as music can prompt forgotten ideas and experiences in all of us, so the memory can be prompted through a rhythmical, phonological approach to issues such as reading, writing and maths. Sing or chant or clap – but link it to a particular concept. But make sure that you don't do this in an obtrusive manner. Encouraging the whole of the back row to stand on the chairs and recite the major rivers of France in the manner of a football chant is unlikely to endear you to the head of geography.

- Ask your dyspraxic learner to repeat the task to you before they begin. Don't encourage them to wait for you to remind them of what they have to do, because in such a way you will encourage them to become passive and disengaged. They must take initiative and ownership.

- It is always helpful to establish a predictable routine and firm guidelines. Sudden changes in routine can cause major problems for a child with dyspraxia. Your presence will be the sort of constant that will provide such predictability. Of course this means that you can never, under any circumstances, be ill or have any sort of other life that might take you away from school, as far as the dyspraxic is concerned.

- A dyspraxic child might need additional time to complete a task satisfactorily. This again is a really important part of your job. You know what the task was, so you can meet with the learner on another occasion to continue with it. I would regard this as vital. If anything is going to help the dyspraxic learner to succeed, it is the fact that someone else was there in the lesson and can provide them with a direct and personal contact with both the subject matter and the task. They can do extra work at lunchtime and after school in a purposeful way with your help. This makes the lesson longer.

- A teaching assistant must stay alert to the learner's needs. The dyspraxic child may find it difficult to wait for the teacher's attention but that shouldn't be an issue, since you are there as an additional adult in the room, so be ready to seize the moment. Quickly reinforce what the teacher has said. Get the child engaged. Make sure they get on the train before it pulls out of the station. Just as it is with many learners, it is getting started that's the problem. Once they have understood and have started the task, it will flow more easily.

- A dyspraxic child with low self-esteem may naturally gravitate towards the back of the classroom. But sitting at the front will help concentration by reducing intrusive distractions. Be ready to force the issue, even if the teacher does not seem prepared to do so.

- Remember that dyspraxic learners are emotionally fragile. They might be unable to deal with disapproval or criticism within the context intended. It won't be their inability in Science that will be criticized. It will be every part of their being. So a careless or casual word could provoke a disproportionate response. You need to stay calm – and learn to manage your own feelings of guilt when an unguarded word leaves them devastated. You will inevitably upset your dyspraxic learner unintentionally. And their parents will do it as well. What you will need to do is play a part in the long task of helping them develop a more robust perspective.

- Always make sure that other teaching assistants are fully briefed about any particular issues, so that they can substitute for you in the classroom, if necessary.
- A learner may be unable to retain learning consistently and the disruption caused by problems such as handwriting, reading and following instructions may obscure the child's intellectual potential. You will need to be their advocate, to make sure that they are not casually and unhelpfully labelled.

Fighting the cause

As time goes on, you will be an advocate for all those with dyspraxia for you will play a major part in releasing their potential. The sad reality is that they can be overlooked.

In the frantic activity that makes up a normal day in school, it is all too easy for teachers to forget what they really should remember. Teachers are human and sometimes they get ratty when they shouldn't. All too easily they might condemn a dyspraxic child for things that they have no control over.

If a dyspraxic child forgets things, then it isn't always their fault. An inability to recall stored information is a difficulty in the processes of storing the stuff, rather than of memory. It is certainly not a sign of laziness. Remember how those messages, like frustrated businessmen with crucial appointments, are being re-routed along twisting suburban lines behind a slow engine.

The dyspraxic child probably wants to learn things just as much as the next, but for them learning takes 20 times the normal effort. This is the case whether the child has to learn where the pencils are kept or where the toilets are or whether they are trying to remember the details of Thomas Hardy's poetry. In fact, any information learned may not be reliably recalled. It could get lost in transit for neurological reasons, as we have seen, an idea suddenly shunted into weedy sidings away from the main line. Before you know it, men in dirty overalls have turned up and are taking the wheels off and the idea will never be mobile again. The child shouldn't be blamed for this. Of course it is exasperating, but there is no one who can possibly be blamed for what is happening. And this is why dyspraxic learners need their teaching assistant.

A proper management structure is essential among teaching assistants just as much as it is among the teaching staff. Not only do you need to be involved in staff meetings and seminars, but you should also have your own briefings. They don't need to be long. Ten minutes every morning should be enough, but you need to share information about the learners you are supporting. Someone else might need to pick up issues and there might be important points or developments that you all need to share.

Remember, dyspraxic learners need familiarity and security, so if you are away on a course, another teaching assistant needs to know what's going on. It means that the dyspraxic learner won't need to explain what they are doing. Keeping a planner, indicating what you are working on with the learner would be very useful.

Development activity 17: In the classroom

What sort of role should you adopt in the classroom?

Are there some areas where this might be easier than in others?

Assess where dyspraxic learners sit in the classes that you attend.

Should this be reviewed?

9

Relationships

The more you think about it, the more it becomes clear that the whole of the job of a teaching assistant is about establishing effective relationships. You do this in order to oil the wheels of learning. You can eliminate confusion and conflict by being there, by making sure that an appropriate focus is maintained, by helping both learner and teacher.

But obviously the most important relationships of all are the ones you form with the learners you are asked to support.

It isn't always easy.

Life isn't fair

The dyspraxic learner might resent your presence as a visible sign of their differences. When you are with them they can't hide anywhere; everyone will know they have got a problem. The others around them will know that this learner needs to be supported, without ever knowing the reason why that support needs to be offered. Then the dyspraxic child can be teased, they can become the subject of unwelcome attention.

Remember, it won't be the system or their condition that will be blamed for this, it will be you. Their dyspraxia is like a heavy weight they have to carry with them throughout their life. You are now a symbol of that weight. You are the albatross they yearn to throw overboard.

They will resent you, because you have, for all intents and purposes, become their dyspraxia. Stephanie at the other side of the classroom hasn't got dyspraxia and we know this because she hasn't got a little helper following her around. You are a visible reminder that life isn't fair.

Think for a moment . . .

What sort of comments would you find most hurtful?

How would you react to them?

Building a successful relationship might be a long haul. Don't ever forget that you are the adult in any equation involving a learner. So it is up to you to take the initiative. Be ready to be rejected and ignored, criticized, abused, insulted and hurt. If these things don't happen, then you are very lucky. But as time goes on, most learners will accept most teaching assistants. It all hinges upon the teaching assistant doing a good professional job. Don't allow yourself to be distracted by hostility and awkwardness. You have to be bigger than that. You need to be firm and focused. In such a way you will prove your worth.

Remember who you are

You are not a teacher and you are not expected to be one, but then neither are you the dyspraxic's best mate. Don't tolerate poor or rude behaviour, because this inhibits teaching and learning. So if these things happen, you have to do something. The dyspraxic needs to know that their poor attitude reflects on you and you are not prepared to accept such behaviour. They are letting you down. If you let them walk over you in an attempt to be friendly, then you will achieve nothing at all. And neither will you achieve anything if you are so fierce that you are scary. There is a delicate line to be walked, but remember what you are doing isn't only for now, it is building for the future and that means that it isn't always easy. It is that old cliché: No pain, no gain.

Behaviour is important and because you are in the classroom when learning is taking place, then you must do whatever you can to support it. You are an integral part of the classroom and the business of the classroom is your business.

The learners don't really distinguish you from their teacher. You are an adult in the classroom and adults in the classroom are, in their experience, teachers. So you need to conform to these expectations. They should call you 'miss' or 'sir', because that is what teachers in a classroom are called. It might sound odd to you when you first start, but to the learners around you this is absolutely normal.

But if you do your job successfully, you will move from being a problem to being a solution. Good ideas will help everyone, not just dyspraxics.

Look at this for a simple but effective idea. You decide to support a dyspraxic learner by providing an egg timer. A simple device, but a learner can see exactly how much time they have got left. This will help to develop a sense of time values. Suddenly other children in the class might want one too. It seems like a fun idea. This will help diminish the isolation of the dyspraxic child. Instead of being an object of derision they could become an object of envy. In helping your dyspraxic, you are now helping other children in the classroom as well.

Time for talking

When you are building your relationship with a dyspraxic, you need to invest nothing more complicated than time. It is the most precious of our resources and you must always try to find some. Discuss school and world events, encourage them to read newspapers and to keep themselves informed. This will give a structure for conversation and improve their self-esteem. It will allow them to develop a sense of themselves as an informed person whom others want to talk to. It is very simple and you are providing them with an opportunity that others around them haven't got. Suddenly they are different – and for positive reasons.

Never forget: such a relationship with a sympathetic adult might be an effective substitute for more challenging relationships with their peers.

Talking is the key. Through talking we find out about each other, so don't be afraid to offer a little bit of yourself. Not contact details or anything like that, but things that make you a real person. Because you will be a real person who is not a relative or a teacher, who is taking an interest in them and allowing them to share a little bit of your life. It is a privilege and one they will appreciate. They are likely to reciprocate.

You can become an ally and a support in the ever-changing and complicated world of school and encourage them to look beyond it.

So focus on the positive. Always ask questions like, 'What have you learned today?' or 'Tell me one good thing that happened to you yesterday'. The dyspraxic child might not always want to respond. They might not wish to be positive. But you must do it. Keep on setting a positive agenda. Always shift the focus to good things. At all costs, you must force them to improve their belief in themselves.

A safe haven

I believe that dyspraxic learners, and others, would gain enormously from a structured environment into which they could retreat. This would be very useful at lunchtime, for a dyspraxic child will often spend this period avoiding things. Give them a time when they can come; give them a place where they can meet. This sort of space in the day can be really useful and you need to liaise with your SENCO about setting up such a club, if you haven't got one already. It will become a haven away from the unattractive jungle of aggressive play or games. Why should they forever be condemned to the fringes of the playground?

This will obviously be an important opportunity to develop a relationship and to find out generally what is going on. Dyspraxic children will need a moment or two to understand what happened in the morning and get ready for the afternoon. 'Have you got your French homework? What have you got to take to maths? Forgotten your ruler? Here's one – but bring it back to me later.' With an older learner say 'Let's look at what is in the newspaper today'.

Other things can come out of such a forum – an understanding of a pupil's interests and a means of exploiting them, for example. They will have a secure place in which they can feel confident enough to share their problems and fears.

Of course, as they get older, then this time can be used very profitably to complete coursework assignments, because they might need a little more time to present things successfully. Ensure access to a computer for use at this time. Other resources like newspapers and magazines could be very useful. I have written more about this idea later on, in the Secondary education section.

Think about handwriting

One thing to remember is that time is made available in the primary school for the development of basic skills like handwriting, but that as learners get older there is often no time set aside for these things. The assumption is made that these skills have been acquired already, and if they haven't, then they can't be improved. What the school requires from handwriting is speed and legibility. You can find the time needed to practice handwriting. However much word processors appear to dominate, they have yet to replace handwriting completely.

It doesn't have to be repetitive exercises in letter formation. It could be the copying out of an important piece of text or an interesting news item. Pursue that interest in the wider world and it will reinforce an enthusiasm or interest with your help. It might be flags or coins or cars. Essentially, what you are doing is giving space and time. There is nothing that is more precious and nothing more important.

**Development activity 18:
A safe haven**

If you had the opportunity to set up a safe haven for dyspraxic learners, what facilities would it need?

Where would it be sited?

When would it be available?

How would it be staffed?

Write it up as a proposal, if you think it appropriate, and show it to your line manager for comments.

10

Organizing

The fate of a dyspraxic learner is to seek desperately for an elusive moment of calm and stillness at the heart of a chaotic world. Everything revolves at high speed. Information bombards them. Demands are piled upon instructions, in a life full of requests and alternatives. They spend their days grasping at things that are no longer there. To be honest, it doesn't appear to be much different for the rest of us. Our own lives appear manic and chaotic at times, but we develop ways of handling this. We have our own ways of getting through the day. Look at how we manage to get out of the house in the morning to go to work. We do it generally because we are organized and because we have a system. Without it, everything will just fall apart. Well, that's what dyspraxics need: a bit of organization. It is something that they often cannot provide for themselves. So you can help them to get organized. And while organizing your own life might seem impossible at times, sorting out theirs is not that difficult.

Leading by example

It's clear that you don't have to take complete control of their life. You are not some sort of secondary brain that takes over when times are hard, via a set of jump leads. You exist to point students in the right direction, through advice and example. You yourself need to turn up to lessons fully equipped and on time, with a clear idea of what is happening and with a clear plan for the whole of the day. This is how you can set an example, and it is important. You must accept that you are a role model. Of course the child needs to begin to take some responsibility for the things around them, because this is the way that they will need to approach the rest of their lives. But a little bit of help at an early age can go a long way.

The importance of planning and management

A carefully arranged strategy by which the dyspraxic child can confront and conquer the school day will help enormously. Someone with your perspective can help to establish a successful and organized routine. Because if learning is to take place, then the challenges presented by the daily business of school need to be resolved. And without a careful and thoughtful approach, the whole day can become a mess.

In fact, it seems to me that effective management of dyspraxia can be achieved in simple things like personal support and organization. Because you can provide the techniques and the structures that they need and, in doing so, you will assist teaching and learning.

Strategies

- A transparent pencil case is very useful. It provides a quick and easy check that everything is in place, without the need for fumbling with uncooperative zips. Such a stylish storage solution is also insisted upon by examination boards; they are the only cases permitted in the exam room. So start early.

- Encourage the learner to have a place for everything and to put things back properly so that they can be easily found. I suppose this is a good analogy for the idea of what is happening inside the dyspraxic's brain. We always need to put things back in the correct place if we want to find them again.

- Encourage the making of lists of things to do that are then regularly reviewed. This is particularly useful with older dyspraxics, but it is obviously something that can be adapted for younger ones too. Start good habits early.

- Use a sloping surface for writing to assist clarity and neatness. An older learner can try this out in a graphics office or you can build a temporary support on a desk from books.

- Post-it notes are very useful. They can provide instant temporary reminders and can be displayed prominently and in a variety of places. Also, they have the advantage of being disposable. Tear them up and start again, or discard them, as a visible symbol of how a learner is moving through a task and nearing its completion.

- Remind teaching colleagues to ask dyspraxic learners to repeat instructions. They should never assume that the child has engaged with the task straight away. It helps if the teacher does this as well as the assistant, not least because it is useful support for others in the class.

- Once you have got to know the learner and have won their confidence, encourage them to join appropriate groups and school societies. It might help – or it might not – on the first couple of occasions to go along with them just to give them the comfort of your support, but that should not persist.

Think for a moment . . .

What sort of organizational hints and systems do you employ in your own domestic life?

Could these be appropriate for anyone else?

Would they be applicable in different circumstances?

Are they suitable for a dyspraxic learner?

- Use a laptop where possible, since it aids correction and redrafting and brings the pleasure of seeing something with a clean professional finish that transcends the vagaries of handwriting.
- The use of a voice recorder can help in remembering important points and instructions. It means that the important points of the lesson are transportable and can be recalled accurately away from the lesson and on other occasions. With the teacher's permission, the use of an MP3 player can be extremely helpful, for many allow voice recording and facilitate discreet playback. This will also provide a structure for written responses, confirming the shape that is required.
- Encourage the child to talk themselves through a task so that they can engage with the different stages and processes that make it up. This will encourage ownership of the task.

This sort of underpinning will allow dyspraxic learners to function both in school and beyond. To see a role model like yourself giving this sort of advice is very influential. It will give weight and credibility to the advice you offer, especially if you are seen as organized and efficient yourself. You will be establishing techniques and processes that should last them a lifetime.

**Development activity 19:
A morning checklist**

Develop a checklist that could be useful for a dyspraxic learner when getting ready for school in the morning.

Offer this to the learner's parents.

Review it after a month.

How useful has it been?

In what ways can it be improved?

11

Behaviour and bullying

A great deal of the daily life of school is about persuading others to do things that they would rather not. No wonder behaviour is such a big issue. When you think about it, much of what happens in our schools is, frankly, peculiar. For example, at a time when their hormones are telling boys they should be climbing trees and wrestling with lions, we try and make them sit down and explore the properties of the equilateral triangle: completely unnatural. It can turn parts of the school day into a never-ending struggle, a battle of wills. Is it any wonder that behaviour has such a prominent profile? Any adult working in a school will eventually find themselves dealing with awkward and difficult young people. It is the way of the world. You cannot be separated from these things.

Think for a moment . . .

What recollections do you have of challenging behaviour from when you were in school?

How were they dealt with?

What sort of behaviour makes you most angry?

What is the most unpleasant incident you have witnessed recently?

Who do you know who has the most effective ways of dealing with challenging behaviour?

What do they do that makes them so successful?

Challenging behaviour has as many different causes as there are troubled learners. With some there is a social or family dysfunction that leads to a rejection of school and its values. In a dyspraxic learner there is a neurological one.

Why would a dyspraxic child reject learning?

As you will be beginning to see, for some dyspraxics school is a daily confrontation with inadequacy. They know they can't cope very well – and they have to face this every day. Not only that, but they are constantly reminded of their shortcomings by other learners and by unsympathetic adults. It is not a satisfactory experience and they are forced to repeat it, seemingly without end. Most of us, when faced with something so unpleasant, would avoid it if it were possible. This is how some dyspraxics feel about education: not as an opportunity for success but as a reminder of failure.

There is an obvious internal tension within dyspraxics because of the difference between what they want to do and what they can achieve. They can model what they want to do quite successfully within their heads. They can imagine themselves as achievers, but it might be some time before reality catches up with their expectations – and there will be others around them who won't let them forget it.

Dealing with other people is also very frustrating for them, and their condition can lead to real exclusion by their peers and a similar lack of understanding from adults. If, for example, they have a difficulty in following instructions, a request for them to be repeated could mean that they are accused of not listening. They can become frustrated and irritated by such perceived intolerance. If they can't keep up with the conversation around them and are mocked for their clumsy interactions, they can feel humiliated and isolated.

The inability to concentrate can lead to similar unfortunate labelling. That is why knowledge about the condition should be shared with others. When, for example, you are supporting a learner, explaining why you are offering this support is a very effective way of raising awareness with new staff or supply teachers.

The stress of being at school can lead to poor behaviour in response to such an unsympathetic world. Indeed, some children can display temper tantrums because the world seems deliberately to misunderstand their condition. They might also carry with them a sense of guilt, because they feel that they are letting their family down because of the way others see them – as a clumsy incompetent embarrassment. No one else in their family has such a reputation.

As they progress through secondary school many dyspraxic students will decide to opt out of education at the earliest opportunity. This shouldn't be a surprise. If they feel that their needs are neither recognized nor met, they can feel isolated and forgotten. It is much easier to be a clown or to become a disaffected isolate in order to hide any limitations and thus avoid dealing with failure.

Recognition

We are always ready to recognize the needs of the physically disabled. Ramps and lifts are rightly provided in schools for children in wheelchairs. No one would expect a deaf child to respond instantly to whispered commands. We would make sure that their needs were met and the necessary equipment made available.

Dyspraxic learners have the same rights. Their condition needs to be recognized and a strategy developed to accommodate it.

A teaching assistant should be an integral part of that strategy. Through the intensive support that you provide, you should attempt to set a positive agenda. This must be the best way of addressing concerns about behaviour. Shouting at a dyspraxic is hardly likely to effect long-term improvement. The nature of your job means that you have more effective ways of modifying behaviour.

Support the child, modify their behaviour and the behaviour of others, and so allow them to succeed.

Be positive

Emphasis needs to be placed upon success rather than failure. Remind them constantly of their achievements. This is a common theme throughout this book: be positive. Your objective must be to disperse the low self-esteem that develops among some dyspraxic children. You can address bullying issues by promoting self-worth.

- Make them feel good about themselves by helping them to be organized.
- Be an organized role model yourself.
- Help them to structure their day.
- Set short-term and achievable goals.
- Encourage their interests.
- Provide a haven for them.
- Introduce them to other learners with whom they can be mutually supportive.
- Be ready to express your disapproval of their more challenging behaviours.
- Contact parents yourself to discuss behaviour issues. Don't ask others to do it because it will undermine your own position. You will also strengthen your position in this way.
- Act as an intermediary between the learner and the teacher if necessary.
- Promote knowledge about dyspraxia.
- Become involved in the lessons yourself.
- Involve non-dyspraxics in your classroom solutions to dispel the sense of isolation.

Victims

There is a reality we must acknowledge and confront. Children with dyspraxia don't go to school on their own. They do not inhabit a vacuum. They go to school with lots of other children, and they try to run where the pack runs, usually with limited success. Where this ends up is that dyspraxic children are frequently the victims of bullying, because often the pack will turn upon them. What parents soon begin to feel is that the dyspraxic child appears to have the word 'Victim' painted on their forehead.

It is a sorry state of affairs indeed, and there is no doubt that the issue of bullying will eventually come your way. Your relationship with the learner might well mean that it is revealed to you before anyone else. You might see it in the corridors or in the classroom. The pencil sharpener that your learner was so pleased to lend as a symbol of friendship comes back broken, a book is damaged, unkind graffiti appears. Or you might see it in the tears.

Why should this happen? Why are dyspraxic children so frequently the victims of bullying?

The answer lies in the nature of their dyspraxia, its consequences, and the way that the dyspraxic child is perceived.

In particular, dyspraxia excludes boys from such defining male activities as running, climbing, kicking and squabbling. They can become loners and, once isolated, easily picked on. Where will you find them in the playground? Around the edge. Where are the pack leaders? In the middle.

The bullying will almost certainly begin in a verbal form as a response to their perceived oddness but it can soon take on physical expression, simply because there is often nothing to stop it from doing so: Hit them. They can't hit you. They can't chase you.

Think for a moment . . .

What sorts of bullying did you see when you were at school?

Are there any differences in what you see today?

It is quite likely that a dyspraxic child will be regarded as peculiar, simply because they don't fit stereotypes. It won't be articulated in this way, but it will appear to their peers that they have not achieved the proper milestones. So their ability to look untidy, their hair, their posture, their walk, can all flash out signals.

What they are just doesn't add up. Their written work can resemble a disaster; their work displayed on the wall, as a gesture towards inclusion, can inspire derision. Yet their general knowledge can be exceptional. So they might be seen as odd, as unexplainable, as freaks. It is seen as best to avoid them because what they have might be catching. The dyspraxic's inability to control their emotions may lead to them being labelled as immature. This can be exacerbated by their obvious difficulties in basic areas like getting dressed, tying laces, eating. They don't conform to basic stereotypes.

It is also possible that they prefer playing with children who are either younger or older than themselves. Their own peers are the ones they avoid because of the challenges they pose – and they are the ones who establish reputations.

I'm dyspraxic. Laugh at me

Dyspraxic learners seem to be living to a different time from the rest of us, always that little bit behind. This is something that comedians have used for years – the character who is out of step, either mentally or physically, with everyone else around them. This comic model is well established. It brings easy laughs.

It can't be a surprise, therefore, if those who fit into this stereotype are derided and abused. They can find themselves the butt of everyone's attempts at humour because they always seem to be catching up with a world that is moving faster than they are. They can say the wrong thing, they can miss the point, they can need three attempts to start a sentence. By the time they get round to finishing it, the world has long since moved on.

Yet it is also true to say that dyspraxic children are special, with a refreshing innocence and an engaging relationship with their work. They must not be sacrificed to the mindless oafs with an old joke to try out. Teachers and teaching assistants will need to show vigilance if dyspraxics are to be given the space in which to succeed. Not to do so is to leave their potential unfulfilled and the world a much poorer place.

The emotional consequences of dyspraxia do need careful consideration. The world they try to inhabit can be difficult enough. Their days can be stressful. They live with frustration, anxiety and failure. Their self-esteem can be low. They may have behaviour problems that these issues provoke. Being dyspraxic is hard work.

The inconsistent development of the brain can affect their emotional development too. The information they get from their experiences and senses may be impaired, so they may not be able to understand their feelings. They may show inappropriate emotions, or too much. So a small set-back can become a disaster. They can be too easily moved to tears. They can focus obsessively upon events like birthdays or holidays, repeating plans and ideas constantly until they appear to be real. They may pursue the repetition of questions and their answers as they try to fix an issue in their minds. This means that ordinary life, as we all come to understand it, can contain additional frustration and disappointment. These frustrations can make them seem immature and certainly emotionally fragile.

Without the consistent ability to read people and situations or to recognize accepted behaviour, friendships may be difficult to form. So on the one hand they want to keep up with their peers and to achieve, but their behaviour seems odd and off-putting. In these circumstances, it is no surprise that they are frequently the victims of prolonged bullying.

We must not let it happen.

Identifying bullying

In the end, what dyspraxic children are is different. And sometimes the others in the pack will want to drive them out. As a concerned and informed adult, you want to harness their potential and offer fulfilment and purpose that will transcend their difficulties. All some of their peers will want to do is to bite them.

You should watch out for the obvious signs that bullying might be happening:

- the child walking alone in the playground;
- the child who is isolated on school visits;
- a shortage of Christmas cards;
- not being invited to parties;
- others being reluctant to sit by them;
- unexplained bruises and scratches;
- possessions frequently disappearing;
- a sudden deterioration in the quality of work and in verbal responses.

Dealing with it

The dyspraxia might be the cause of the bullying but the solutions and strategies that need to be adopted are no different from those employed in any other circumstances.

Your institution should have established and clear-cut rules about how it should be dealt with. You need to be familiar with the school's bullying policy. A support network needs to be provided and a mentoring scheme established. Remember, a dyspraxic learner will usually relate well to someone who is older. That someone might be you. Your job is to develop a supportive relationship so that they feel confident enough to talk to you about such issues. But, of course, never take the law into your own hands, as much as you might think it justified.

You must implement the bullying policy of the place where your work. To do otherwise makes you no better than the bully.

There is undoubtedly a touching level of sadness in life with a dyspraxic. Whatever they want always seems just outside their grasp. They need to be protected. Theirs is a hard enough road as it is.

**Development activity 20:
Bullying**

Obtain and read a copy of the bullying policy.

Write a series of bullet points outlining the key points which can be displayed on the wall, if there isn't already one there.

What are your responsibilities within this policy?

Does the policy include sections on the different sorts of bullying, including cyber-bullying?

Talk to dyspraxic learners about the policy. What do they think?

12

Specific hints and tips

It is time now to look at particular parts of the school system to see precisely what sort of support a teaching assistant can offer a dyspraxic learner. This is not an exhaustive list. All it can ever do is to point you in the right direction. The ideas that you come up with to solve specific challenges in your own classrooms will always be far more effective than anything you try to copy from a book. I merely hope that these tips offer you some sense of direction. Use them of course, because that is why they are here; but, more importantly, adapt them. Don't think about the children I know; think about the children you know and work with. It is a creative activity and an enjoyable one.

There are no barriers here. A lot of the advice isn't relevant to only one particular stage of education; it should be regarded as being transferable from one stage to another. A dyspraxic child's requirements don't necessarily change when they move between schools and stages. The condition does not respect the artificial barriers that we have created. So it may be that ideas that can help are outside the age range of the learner with whom you are concerned. A learner at any age could still have all the problems presented by a pre-school child with little or no improvement. The emphasis in whatever you do must be on providing the strategy that is most appropriate to support learners and their learning at that time.

Of course, the demands made upon you may vary, but the most important demand of all is the requirement to find strategies that will enable a dyspraxic child to achieve more than they would if you were not there at all.

Pre-school and nursery

At this stage parents are probably most worried about the erratic development of their dyspraxic child. They won't be achieving the same milestones as easily as the children of the other parents in the playground who always boast so much of their child's genius. Nothing seems right and little is explained. The child they love so much seems to be a freak. Why? What will the future hold for them? If you are working with dyspraxic children at this time, then the feelings of parents will be at their most raw. But they will certainly want to do something – anything – to re-wire their child. We know this is not possible, but if and when dyspraxia is diagnosed, then you will be able to offer reassurance. A label brings with it strategies. And books.

You should propose activities that will provide a bridge between home and school. These will show that we are all together and that we are all committed to effecting an improvement. This will have a very positive effect on parents. They won't feel alone. You should find enjoyable activities that the child wants to do. The sort of things you can do at this stage will not reflect the formality of learning that emerges later. Here the emphasis falls upon focused and structured play that will have long term benefits, both in social and physical development. Think of children's games.

- You can encourage parents and carers to use any poems or songs which have actions, such as 'Simon Says . . .'. This helps copying, listening skills and body awareness.
- Other games, like 'Incy Wincy Spider', 'Heads, shoulders, knees and toes', or 'In a cottage in a wood', are very good for developing finger dexterity and fitting the speed of the actions to the speed of the song, as well as for body awareness.
- A game like 'Pass the Parcel' helps laterality by promoting an awareness of 'passing to the side' and then promotes

fine motor skills when the parcel has to be unwrapped, with an added sense of excitement.

You should emphasize the fantasy and emotional elements of their play. This will encourage them to do more, since they will then concentrate upon the artificial world and its implications, rather than the mechanics of performance. They will be allowing their instinctive actions to take over, which will be more efficient. It will encourage success and confidence. Modelling stories and actions with figures or toys will encourage purposeful movements.

Join in with their activities. Sometimes don't ask questions or make demands, but rather follow the instructions they give you. They will benefit from having to direct your part in it through clear instructions. They will see the consequences of the things they suggest.

Physical activities are very important at this time, to encourage awareness of where body parts are positioned at any particular time. Games which include 'space' or 'direction' words can be very valuable. 'Go under your partner's legs or climb through the barrel. Go onto the top of the box then jump down and come back to the start.' You are reinforcing a sense of direction and of order.

In fact, you can work with the teacher and ask the child to help build an obstacle course to develop such skills. The planning and the building will help organizational abilities and promote self-confidence. It will help them to learn how to judge distances and examine the consequences of what they do. The obstacle course itself will help to develop motor abilities. The child has to distribute their body weight in different ways, as well as adjust the speed and effort they must put into a specific action or movement.

Naturally you will be on hand to help them succeed. You can give a commentary as they negotiate the circuit. 'You are very good at climbing. Now tell me how you are going to get down.'

Development activity 21: Obstacle course

Design an obstacle course for use in your school, using the resources that are readily available.

In anything that you do with dyspraxic learners, always allow for repetition and practice. They will need this time to firm up the skills they are trying to acquire.

Much of what you do will provide a secure foundation for what will happen later in the child's school career. You can put in place simple things that will have a huge influence later on. You can begin to improve the quality of movement, for example, and develop greater confidence in spatial awareness. You will help the brain to refine and improve the connections that need to be made.

You are part of a long, slow process, but slight improvements will eventually combine to produce noticeable benefits. The activities chosen must be simple enough to allow the child to succeed but structured to bring about both progress and understanding.

Some of the things that work are really simple and children enjoy them because success is easily measured and perceived. Jumping over a line between cones and placed at differing heights can be a good way to start.

All these things are inclusive activities. Everyone can take part. Their success is not really dependent upon impressive physical attributes. By helping to direct the child's play and movement you are giving them the support they need and making them feel better about themselves.

The primary phase

What does a dyspraxic parent want from a primary school?

First and foremost, they want a school with a uniform that has no ties, no laces and no buttons. These simple things can be a real nightmare for dyspraxic learners and their parents. This desire is an indication of how much more complicated the process of going to school becomes as learners get older.

Arriving in primary school itself is a significant moment of change. New people, new structures, new furniture to bump into. It can be a very unsettling experience. A well-informed teaching assistant will make a big difference.

You can offer specific and supportive advice about managing the school experience for their child. You are very well placed to do this because your role allows you to offer personal and specific support. If you sort out these issues, then learning can more readily take place. So your role initially might be more parent-orientated.

- Advise parents to label clothes clearly.
- Tell parents to choose a school bag with roomy and separate pockets. Then separate out personal items, like lunch, into one pocket and school things, like a pencil case, into another. Always put them in the same place. It will help packing and checking if things have their own special place. A diagonal strap distributes weight more evenly than a strap over one shoulder and helps children who have balancing difficulties.
- They should look for Velcro fastenings on shoes.
- Elasticated waists on shorts and trousers can be helpful. Pleated trousers make it easier to distinguish the front from the back.
- Personal hygiene could be a problem. An electric tooth-brush will aid efficiency.
- If a child suffers when their hair is combed or brushed, then advise that it is kept short.

- While you will be naturally aware of child protection issues, you will use discreet assistance when necessary, to other children as well as dyspraxics, in order to minimize personal issues. Reminders to go to the toilet at appropriate moments and to wash hands afterwards will help to avoid embarrassment.

- The child may not leave enough time to get to the toilet. They may not recognize the signals soon enough, so that by the time they get there they might be in a bit of a rush. If you add on the tricky business of getting trousers up and down, then you will see that the potential for accidents is extensive.

- The processes involved in wiping the bottom might be difficult to coordinate. So the opportunities for embarrassment are huge and as a result you might try to avoid the experience altogether. One of the results can be constipation. You might want to discuss with parents the idea of establishing a regular toileting regime. 'Let's get it out of the way before we go to school, shall we?'

- Problems with hand-washing will be greatly helped by the provision of wet-wipes.

- Eating in school could be a real problem. Cutlery may still be difficult to master and a child could become particularly self-conscious. So perhaps sandwiches are a better practical alternative. It would be better to wrap them in foil rather than use cling film, which can be difficult to deal with. Firm sandwich fillings like cheese are easier to handle than sloppy ones. Make sure that pre-wrapped food can be unwrapped easily.

- Suggest that parents provide drinks that don't need pouring. Boxes of juice with a straw are a simple solution, just so long as the child does not squeeze the box against their body, thus spraying juice everywhere.

The dyspraxic child may have managed to avoid certain activities in playgroup or nursery as a way of hiding their difficulties. They will have known for some time that some things are rather tricky. However, as the curriculum becomes more structured and formal, they will have to confront their problems. They will have to deal with large amounts of new and confusing information and more specific physical demands. The developmental gaps between children will widen – and conclusions will be drawn about those who can't carry out particular activities with confidence, such as dressing, eating and other domestic tasks. Catching a ball will assume far more importance than it should.

The child may have significant issues to face and one of the functions you will perform is to support the child and to suggest remedial actions. As the child gets older they should become more involved in working out appropriate strategies.

When you have spent some time in a primary classroom, you will realize that it is a busy and noisy place, in the middle of which the dyspraxic child is supposed to sit still. It isn't the easiest place to negotiate. They may, for example, find themselves sitting with their back to the teacher for part of a lesson. They will have to maintain attention while dodging backwards and forwards to follow the focus of the topic. They will have difficulty in listening and in following instructions, especially if the teacher moves around into different parts of the room while they are speaking.

One of your major tasks will be to ensure that messages are received and understood. You will need to promote focus and concentration. You will be a mediator. You will be setting short-term achievable goals in order to support learning. You can work on particular exercises targeted to make a positive impact. You will always find that dyspraxic children enjoy the individual attention you provide and can thrive in situations where they are not competing with their peers. I suppose it is compensation for playground neglect. They crave acceptance and enjoy responsibility. Being with a teaching assistant is a time when they can find both these things.

Primary school can be a tough time for dyspraxic children and their parents. What you can do is to show that no one has to accept things as they are. You can do things that really will make things better. And, as small improvements add together through repeated practice, then significant progress will be gradually noted.

Of course, as the child progresses through the school, their ability to deal with different situations will improve – of course it will. A dyspraxic child isn't fixed forever within an unresponsive body. They do change, they do develop naturally, though perhaps at a slower rate. The remedial exercises suggested should eventually have an impact. So the child will change, their confidence in some situations will improve, their concentration and focus will develop. It is just a longer process. But you will have contributed to this. A good teaching assistant can then take a sense of professional pride in the positive changes that they have inspired.

Development activity 22:
Practical solutions

Design a parental checklist and advice sheet offering practical solutions.

Show it to a senior colleague for their comments.

Distribute it to parents and ask them to assess its relevance at the end of the year.

Amend as necessary.

Classroom management

So what are the kinds of things that you can suggest that will assist teaching and learning in the classroom?

- One of the most important things that a teaching assistant can do is to make sure that the dyspraxic child sits facing the teacher as much as possible. Maintaining eye contact can be an important aid to concentration. You will be there to help maintain such a focus.
- Instructions might need to be broken down into smaller and more easily digestible steps. When the class receives instructions, you can plan out a strategy that involves small but incremental stages. Gently repeat things when necessary.
- Ask the child to repeat the instructions given, to reinforce understanding. You might need to plan written responses carefully in order not to overwhelm the child with the amount of handwriting required.
- Your expectations should be communicated clearly and concisely. You must not employ extreme or false praise, because in the end we all learn to see through this, but always try to be encouraging.
- One of the big differences you can make is that you are immediately on hand to deal with issues. In other circumstances dyspraxic learners would find it very difficult to wait for adult attention because it would be hard to keep a grip on the ideas or questions they wish to express.
- The child will need a predictable routine, as sudden changes could be particularly unsettling. You will be part of that routine, to the extent that to begin with, at least, they will not be willing to try anything unless you are there. In the long term, your objective must be to ensure that there will come a point at which they can work independently. So you are not trying to develop a situation in which you become indispensable. You are actually aiming towards independence.

Dyspraxic children have many valuable intellectual strengths which mean that they can contribute in an effective way in group situations. This can be an important way of improving self-esteem and the way in which they are seen by their peers. So always make sure that the dyspraxic child is fully involved in all group activities. Group work can build important bridges between children if the groups are selected sensitively. Once they are working in a group, you can take more of a withdrawn role. But you need to observe what's going on so that you can reflect and comment upon it later.

Homework

Perhaps an important element in this process towards independent learning is to be found in the increasing demands for the completion of homework. However, homework does give the dyspraxic child some difficulties. They may have to concentrate and work much harder than others in the class. This means they may be very tired by the time they get home. At this point they are expected to do more of what they found difficult in the first place.

It is a challenging issue – because they don't want to be singled out by not doing the homework. At the same time, they could feel totally overwhelmed by the tasks, particularly since they are asked to attempt these exercises without the support of their teaching assistant.

The most important thing you can do is to help them get organized.

- A homework diary needs to be kept.
- A prominently displayed planner at home and in the classroom can help by indicating regular tasks and deadlines.
- The use of kitchen timers and stopwatches can be used to counteract poor time-awareness. This technique can be used both at school and at home.

- Tasks can be planned and the amount of time they need could be predicted. This will give them an important idea about how long a particular task will take.
- Tasks can be simplified and broken down into small achievable stages.

**Development activity 23:
Homework**

Design a useful homework planner that would help a dyspraxic learner to manage their homework tasks effectively.

Planning and organization

In order to carry out this important level of support, it is essential that the teaching assistant knows in advance what sort of topics will be presented during lessons and as homework assignments, so that you can plan the support that a dyspraxic learner requires. A high level of cooperation between teacher and assistant will offer a genuine possibility of improvement over time. You will be working together to develop a strategy to achieve shared goals. You are equal partners in this strategy. Without each other you would be so much poorer and so much less effective. Here are some other useful hints that might help in the classroom.

Writing

A dyspraxic child may not have developed an appropriate tripod grip for writing. Their grip might weaken quickly or they may apply too much pressure in order to maintain control. Handwriting can thus appear uneven and crude. It might not be possible to write along a line or to keep words separate. Letter formation might not be consistent. Writing at the top of the page could be better than that at the bottom.

You might see this before anyone else and it is important for your credibility, with both leaner and teacher, that you are in a position to offer immediate practical advice in the classroom.

- Experiment and try to find a pen that the child finds easy to hold. There are lots of pens around these days – with foam grips or with textured barrels, for example. Triangular-shaped pens are sometimes a successful solution.

- If written work is sometimes too untidy, then allow the use of a pencil, just as long as the child does not repeatedly press down too hard and so snap the lead. Mistakes can be easily erased and the finished product will look more acceptable to the child. But you must always be aiming towards the more consistent use of a pen. A pencil cannot be a permanent solution.

- Inclined boards for reading and writing can make an enormous difference. These can be simply improvised if funds are short. They help to ease visual tracking from the board or screen to the exercise book because the eyes do not need to drop so far. They also ease pressure on the wrist during writing. An inclined board also helps reading because the eyes, apparently, are less likely to jump over letters since the angle helps to achieve a focus. You can improvise a board to begin with, before you arrange for more permanent ones to be made or provided, once you have shown that they work.

- Fix paper or books to the boards with masking tape if necessary. This ensures that the book does not wobble and helps handwriting. Again, it is a short-term solution, but an important one.

- Make sure that overhead lights don't glare or reflect directly on the child's work. This makes visual difficulties worse. Be prepared to move the learner.

- Experiment by playing Mozart in class as an aid to concentration, as long as you have the agreement of the teacher. It might sound daft, but they do say that it works.
- A computer can help to make work presentable, and makes the work of a dyspraxic child indistinguishable from the work of anyone else. Computer skills are important for the future anyway. You will certainly have to make sure that your own skills are up to the mark!
- A child does still need to acquire some facility in handwriting. However difficult they might find it, writing can't be replaced entirely. Repetitive exercises on letter formation can be employed as a means of slowly improving handwriting. But writing out a favourite poem or piece from a story can be more fun and reinforces an emphasis upon learning. You can also encourage the development of a particular interest by providing suitable material to be turned into some kind of presentation.
- Be careful if you need to ask for untidy work to be done again. The child will know that repetition usually means that something was wrong in the first place. It is better to talk about 'redrafting' and 'final copies'. Without such sensitivity, the child's sense of failure could be continually confirmed, switching them off from education entirely. Your role isn't about punishment but about improvement.
- Oral storytelling for story-writing or having the children tape-record their stories so that they can be written a few sentences at a time can be a useful approach. Voice recorders are now a part of so many communication devices.
- Don't be afraid to take the child into another environment where they can concentrate without other distractions. Once the task has been established, then sometimes a spell outside or in the library will help. Don't do it all the time, but it is a useful strategy to employ.

Music

Music has an important part to play in everyone's education. It stresses a sense of order and sequence. The consequences of disorder are instantly apparent. However, learning to play the recorder, which is an important part of the primary experience, can be difficult if you don't have reliable, fine control of the fingers. A triangle or tambourine would be better alternatives. Repeating patterns and structures in increasingly complex forms could be very beneficial. It is something that you should encourage. In this way, then, the child could be included in any ensemble work and be an integral part of it. It will make a huge contribution to the development of self-esteem and be important in encouraging teamwork.

Songs and word games like 'I went to market' can be very successful as a way of teaching memory and sequence. Children enjoy it and want to be part of the fun – and this will encourage concentration and involvement.

Dance

Dance can have a very important part to play, particularly ensemble work. It provides a forum in which to learn about and develop structured movement. When children move together and then apart in a planned way, they develop an awareness of someone else's movement and must adjust their timing and use of space to be part of the overall design. It does sound rather complicated when expressed in this way, but it is essentially all about controlled movement.

Four children can dance together – using movements practised in pairs, adjusting their use of space and so composing a group dance. This could include parts where everyone moves together and actions are performed in sequence. Again, awareness of other children, memorizing the short dance and retaining the quality of the chosen movements provides an enjoyable challenge. Of course, remembering what comes next helps planning and sequencing. Your help could be crucial in developing success.

Think for a moment . . .

Consider how important creative activities can be in improving opportunities for dyspraxic learners. Such activities should never be dismissed as trivial.

Scissors

These might be very hard to use. Holding the paper in one hand and then making the correct open and close movements could be almost impossible. Even if the dyspraxic child can manage to close them, they may not be able to carry out the associated cutting movement. Spring-assisted scissors could reduce coordination difficulties. Starting with firmer paper could help. Cutting squares or rectangles from a long strip is a way of developing skills. This is best practised away from the harsh attention of other class members who may have skills which are more naturally honed. It is, however, going to be a long hard struggle.

There are other activities that can be employed to support improvement in hand control.

Winding a lace round a bobbin is very difficult and is a real test of fine motor skill. It is something that you can slip into quiet moments in the classroom – during wet play or at the end of the day, for example – and it is something that you can very easily initiate. All sorts of threading activities can be very beneficial and there are many commercial variants of this activity that parents can also get involved in to help skills to grow. A nail pattern hammered into wood in the form of a spider's web allows children to hold with one hand and wind wool with the other. This helps coordination and shows how actions can have creative and unexpected outcomes.

Lego can also help manipulation. Building with bricks helps planning and sequencing. Of course, the bricks don't change shape either: they are the same shape for everyone and your creation has the same components as anyone else.

Hand exercises or the making of shapes with clay or plasticine can warm up the muscles before activities such as writing begin. This is worth pursuing. Screwing loose plastic nuts and bolts together is another obvious activity that helps coordination.

Rulers and other equipment

Using a ruler can be awkward, as it requires the child to hold it down with one hand and to draw with the other. All of us find at one time or another that they seem to move for no good reason. A metal 'safety ruler' with a groove stamped into it, or one with a raised handle or ridge, might help. Make handles for smaller pieces of mathematical equipment with lumps of Blutack. A compass is another tool that is difficult to master. A blob of Blutack into which the point can be placed aids stability and accuracy, but it is never going to be a piece of equipment that a dyspraxic child can master with much consistency.

Sequencing and number

When you consider how the brain might be having difficulty remembering certain actions, it will be no surprise to learn that sequencing activities could be a problem. You can help by using picture stories and asking the child to put them in the right order. If you put things in the wrong order, then your story doesn't make sense, so it has to be reviewed.

It is very useful for dyspraxic children to have lots of estimating games in the classroom – for example, 'How many long steps will you need to place the ball in the box?'; 'Which kind of ball will you choose if you are going to bounce a ball over the box?' The children can estimate and then try! There are important lessons here and the skills in making judgements are important because they involve making decisions and assessing the consequences of any actions.

Another good way to start is with something like 'Sweets in

the jar'. The child must guess the number of sweets or cubes in a jar. They will need to unscrew the lid, empty them out, count them and then fill the jar again. Holding the jar with one hand and unscrewing the lid is a very difficult for a dyspraxic child but it is important that it is practised. At first the children will clamp the jar into their bodies for extra support but with practice they should eventually be able to hold it on the table to unscrew the lid.

Secondary education

All too soon, it might seem, you will be watching the child you have worked with for so long preparing to move on. You will have developed a productive relationship with them and you will probably feel apprehensive about how they are going to cope when they move on to the next stage. They will be exchanging the familiar and the comfortable for uncertainty and anxiety.

But you have an important role to play in making sure they are well prepared for this major change. The more preparatory work you do, the more successful the transition will be. It is going to be difficult, make no mistake about that. But a positive agenda needs to be established. The change is exciting and manageable. Everyone needs to accept this and everyone has a part to play in making it work.

Careful preparations must be made by both parents and by both schools. All children will benefit from effective liaison, but none more so than those who might be experiencing difficulties. Your job as a teaching assistant is to take a mature and positive attitude towards transition.

Sharing information

The secondary school will have procedures in place to receive information from the primary school. This information must be distributed so that all staff are aware. This is an immediate difference between the two institutions. In primary school, children are taught mostly by one teacher; in secondary school they are taught by many. So there are more staff who need to be made aware of essential information. Unguarded comments resulting from lack of information can be embarrassing and hurtful. In fact, a lack of awareness can make teachers look foolish. This is an essential difference in the role of the teaching assistant in the two institutions. You will need to manage a variety of teachers, a new complexity.

So proper liaison provides a bridge between primary and secondary and is designed to ensure there is a continuum linking the two phases. You have a huge part to play in this process. You should at the earliest opportunity find your counterpart in the new school and pass on vital information. It is not only performance details that need to be passed on, but also the additional, personal and quirky information that you have acquired that can make all the difference – their interests, their families, their sensitivities. It should ensure that the earlier good experiences are built upon and the bad ones are not inadvertently repeated.

Information needs to be passed on and the child needs to know that this has happened. It is reassuring for them that in

**Development activity 24:
Liaison**

Design an appropriate proforma on which you could record all the information you believe it would be necessary to pass on to the new teaching assistant.

Fill out an example for a child who you know well.

Does the resulting document look useful?

Show the format to your line manager for their comments.

a way their familiar adults are still watching over them. Dyspraxic children are no different in this than any other. They all have their stories to tell and the secondary school experience will be a better one if we listen properly across the key stages.

If the child is to manage the transition to secondary school with some success, then the process needs to begin before they even arrive. This is, of course, where you feature strongly. What the dyspraxic child needs is familiarity, a gradual introduction to this new phase in their life. So early visits to the school are crucial, both as part of the class and as an individual. You should establish that it is appropriate for you to accompany the child on any preliminary tours of the school.

Teaching assistant? Or tour guide?

I also believe that individual tours can be extremely useful. Dyspraxics, more than most, will need to be prepared for movement around the school and for that bewildering and unexpected sea of faces. Introductions could be made, both to teachers and to the other important members of the school, particularly the teaching assistants with whom they might be working. It is important for the child that these connections have been made. It makes it all seem just a little more familiar. This is an opportunity to find all the important places – the office, the dining hall, the toilets – without the distractions of others.

This process could represent a kind of handing-over. Meet the new faces who will help them; establish points of contact. Teaching assistants provide something fixed and familiar in an ever-changing secondary school.

A lot depends upon the sort of induction programme that has been established and how Learning Advice departments and SENCOs operate. It might be that significant staff will have already visited their partner schools to find things out and to meet significant pupils. This sort of practice blurs the boundaries between the two phases and so makes transition more manageable. Teaching assistants from both sides need to be involved in this.

Living in a different world

Secondary school is very different. Some children thrive straight away. Others take longer to adjust. Children with dyspraxic tendencies might take much longer that most.

For those who crave a simpler life, a secondary school appears deliberately confusing. Instead of a small, contained area where everything is to hand, the learning environment can be a sprawling mass. Certainly there is more specialist equipment but it seems to be spread out everywhere. Going to school now involves moving around in what seems to be a random fashion, in response to a confusing timetable of lessons. Their lasting impression of secondary school could be that of a seething mass of older pupils, all knowing where they are going, so unlike the simpler and neater world of the primary school. Now the registration group will be full of children they do not know. Personal space will not be constant. There will be more than one table or desk where learning can take place.

We want our schools to be interesting and challenging places. Exciting. Vibrant. Yet that also means more opportunities for confusion for a dyspraxic child. Nothing seems certain any more. There seems to be less for them to hold on to.

Teachers

And then there are all those teachers. No longer one but a range of them. It would not, for example, be unusual if they were meeting male teachers for the first time. Some of these teachers may not have any understanding of, or sympathy for, the condition. They may deal rather harshly with a child they regard as lazy or obstructive. Then there might suddenly be a supply teacher covering for someone familiar. Or there will be a teacher who doesn't teach the class very often – say, once a week – and so the gap between lessons can make the work all too confusing and all too forgettable. Different faces, different rooms, different tolerances, different expectations.

Think for a moment . . .

Think about a dyspraxic learner you know.

What would you identify as their most challenging day?

What are the differences in the teachers who they meet during this day?

This should certainly tell you something. That the teaching assistant's role is such a vital one, in providing consistency and familiarity. Teachers may change and will often do so in confusing ways, but your assistant does not. Always there, providing consistent support. This is why they gave you a job.

Getting lost

The child with dyspraxia may feel disorientated and get lost, arriving late to lessons. It will take them much longer to internalize a map and to pattern their movements round the school. If they are separated from the others in their class who they have been following all day, then they could become completely disorientated. Teachers they don't know will shout at them for being in the wrong place when they don't even know where the right place is. The school will seem unfriendly and intimidating, a place designed to be deliberately confusing, a noisy shapeless threat, full of new and unsympathetic demons.

Now they need you more than ever.

Establishing a base

I think that teaching assistants can do something very effective by providing a base and a haven for all dyspraxics in the school. Of course, it may support children with other difficulties too and it will help, among other things, to address those initial difficulties of transition. It will be an ideal place for learners and teaching assistants to meet and build the relationships upon which success will depend.

I think the idea of such a support system is worth exploring because it gives a sense of importance. It should become a permanent base, a stable haven in a constantly changing world. It could be just a place to eat sandwiches. But they will always know that it is there. A bolthole. A home. A place where you can access the help you need; a place where you can go when the going gets tough.

The children can take ownership of this base, decorating it and displaying their work. It is the sort of place they need.

Dyspraxic children will need to take a moment or two to understand what happened in the morning and get ready for the afternoon. It is a place where they can escape the isolation of the schoolyard or the playing fields.

Other things can come out of such a group – an understanding of a pupil's interests and a means of exploiting them, for example. They will have a secure place in which they could feel confident enough to share their problems and fears.

Of course, as they get older, then this time can be used very profitably to complete coursework assignments because they might need a little more time to present things successfully. Ensure access to a computer for use at this time.

Dyspraxics of all ages will be able to meet here. Younger students will watch the older ones working and succeeding, thereby offering support and helping to dispel any sense that they are isolated freaks. Dyspraxics are not alone, and you need to develop a sense of community.

Think for a moment . . .

Think about whether establishing such a haven would be a good idea.

Would it, in your view, exacerbate bullying by making dyspraxic learners more easily identifiable?

What resources would you need?

How much would it cost?

Should you put together a proposal for inclusion in the development plan?

Different subjects

Each subject that is taught in a secondary school brings with it its own expectations and its own rules. This means that they have their own particular and perhaps unexpected difficulties for a dyspraxic learner. I will try in this section to outline specific ideas that a teaching assistant may find useful as they move around a secondary school. I cannot cover all possibilities, I can just give you a flavour. The most important thing I can suggest is that you use your imagination and your commitment to develop strategies that will help the particular learner to whom you are assigned. What I can't cover either are the differences in the personalities and expectations of the teachers in the school. You will have to work this out for yourself, because every school is unique.

Science

Here the seating available, particularly in a laboratory, could make life very difficult for a child with poor balance. They could be concentrating so much on maintaining their balance on a lab stool that they have no idea what is going on in the lesson. Perhaps it would be better for them to stand during any experiments. Indeed, in some experiments, particularly in the early years, the dyspraxic child could be a positive danger. So it might be better to let them watch rather than expose them to danger and ridicule. Someone – the SENCO or the teaching assistant – needs to take the initiative and tell the Science department in order to pre-empt problems. This emphasizes the key point about supporting children with any sort of difficulty – the need for effective communication between professionals.

Don't forget that dyspraxic children need to be part of a team, and the acceptance that this represents. With your help they can find an important role in group activities. They need to. They might begin by recording results, but once they are involved then their role can develop. They can bring lots of positive elements to group work, because they interpret the world in a different way. It gives them unexpected insights and eventually this is a way in which they can establish credibility with other students.

Drama

This is a subject that could help a dyspraxic child enormously. The bright lights of the stage might be too uncomfortable but the opportunity to work behind the scenes in productions or to be involved in improvisation in lessons will help to raise self-esteem. Dyspraxics want to be involved and like the idea of the sort of teamwork that is often denied to them because of their condition. They could be extremely useful production assistants and this will give them pleasure and status. They will learn the importance of schedules and timing and clear preparation and organization. It is something significant and exciting that they can be part of.

English

The subject has significant emotional content, particularly in the study of literature, and can provide an opportunity for the expression of personal feelings and for empathy with characters and situations. It is important to encourage an examination of the feelings of others in the controlled environment that a book provides. An opportunity to focus on ideas and opinions and to contribute on an equal footing in oral exercises is something that they will appreciate. It will help to counteract any difficulties in their standing that confused and untidy handwriting might give them. If such a problem is present, then look for the different ways of presenting and recording achievement that are presented to us through technological developments. The sort of issues that are dealt with in English lessons will provide a teaching assistant with fruitful opportunities for discussion. The opportunity to write about themselves could be very revealing.

Design Technology

The obvious practical emphasis of this subject makes it fraught with difficulty. Inadequate control and manipulation can place us on the cusp of disaster. The prospect of a dyspraxic child with a sharp knife in one hand and a slippery onion in the other can send shivers running down your spine, as can the image of the workshop technician running for the first aid box while the teaching assistant tries to staunch the flow (you might have to do that part for them).

Once again, the opportunity for teamwork could be very important. The dyspraxic child may not have the appropriate manual dexterity but there are contributions that they can make when they are part of a problem-solving team. They will have insights and solutions because they are indeed different. Contributing towards the successful achievement of an objective will help to build bridges between themselves and others. They can be part of a team that succeeds in a way that they never could in a sporting context.

Think for a moment . . .

Think about the important problem-solving elements of Design Technology lessons.

What are the skills have you noticed in these lessons?

What sort of activities could you or other members of your team design that would enable the dyspraxic learner to practise the necessary skills outside the lesson – at lunchtime, for example?

Are there any specific resources you might need?

Would it be appropriate to establish a regular club to support issues like dexterity and teamwork?

Maths

In Maths the dyspraxic child may find it hard to line up columns of figures in order to do calculations. So make sure that they have access to squared paper that will stop figures becoming transposed. Remember that any activity involving scissors could prove exceedingly difficult to perform with any accuracy or precision. Such inabilities are quickly picked up on by those in the classroom who are less than sympathetic. Tracing or mirror work might present unexpected difficulties and have within them the potential for humiliation. Alternative approaches can always be employed. The difficulties we noted in the primary sector don't suddenly go away.

Physical Education

This is a significant subject because it is the area that lies at the heart of the dyspraxic's problems. There should be no doubt at all that PE is a nightmare area for the dyspraxic child. This lesson could prove to be one of the most stressful times of their week.

Other children around them will be achievers. They will have an instinctive grasp of the skills they need to play games.

The dyspraxic child will stand out: certainly ungainly, possibly inept. Their inability will have inevitable consequences. In team games they will be the last to be picked. In the changing room they may well be the first to be picked on.

You have a huge job to do here, in tandem with the teacher. The support you offer is vital. The learner you are supporting will need to establish a healthy physical future and if they reject PE completely, then they might struggle to do so, with all the problems that this might imply.

The PE lesson can hang over them like a black cloud – a constant and public reminder of their inabilities. They won't be indifferent to PE; they will hate it. They will avoid it at any cost, truanting from school if that is the only way to escape the humiliation. Dealing with the impatience of others in team situations will haunt them constantly.

You will realize that the changing rooms will require careful supervision to prevent intimidation and humiliation. You won't be able to go into the changing room, but once you have established a trusting relationship, then the learner will tell you if there are difficulties. Your job then is to tell someone. You will also need to make sure, particularly in the earlier years, that issues about getting dressed and looking presentable once the lesson has ended are resolved as quickly as possible.

The activities involved in the lesson can be very difficult and stressful. Ball skills may be non-existent. Climbing onto benches and apparatus can be daunting. But they must not be humiliated in physical activity. They need encouragement and you must certainly not back away from supporting them in this area. You can take them for quiet and private practice away from unsympathetic eyes at alternative times, not just in scheduled PE lessons. Of course, you might not be trained to undertake specialist activities like swimming; these are issues for subject specialists. But there are other simpler – and enjoyable – things a teaching assistant can do, like skittles. Let's be flexible. Let's be imaginative. Better doing this than sitting in an unproductive lesson, covered by a supply teacher. Take them away and do something better. And there are strategies that you can suggest that will help.

- A dyspraxic child will find kicking a ball very difficult. They will be unable to direct it accurately and will struggle to make judgements about how hard the ball needs to be kicked. Skills can be improved by using a large foam ball to show direction and the amount of force required.

- PE can do a great deal to improve handwriting through the use of directional games, reinforcing the concept of left-to-right movement. It will also help with the concepts of order and direction. Movement to music will also help by giving a structure to movement and so help with the rhythm required for efficient handwriting. You can be involved in such exercises.

- Skittles is an activity that can be beneficial. Rolling a ball to knock down skittles helps aiming and coordination. Alleys can be constructed with benches to contain the ball so that poor aiming isn't immediately apparent by the ball going sideways. Skittles can be made from plastic bottles half-filled with sand, or water if the game is outside. They can then judge and measure how much water has been lost when the skittle falls over. Younger children can make lighter skittles which will topple more easily.

- Basketball can be fun. Waste paper baskets tied to wallbars are excellent for learning to aim and developing a sense of distance and direction. The distance between the child and the basket can, naturally, be varied and a competitive element can be included if you wish.

Development activity 25: Physical education

Speak to the PE specialists in your institution. What simple activities can they suggest that would be appropriate for dyspraxic learners?

What sort of training would you need in order to facilitate these activities successfully?

You will be able to offer the PE department advice about dyspraxic learners. These learners must be nurtured. They must get attention, they should be given significant tasks to perform in lessons. They could become the trusted companion with important responsibilities, the kit-manager, the scorer to the team. But if they are ignored and marginalized, then the institution will be complicit in the resulting bullying.

Getting organized

A carefully arranged strategy to the school day will help enormously, and a teaching assistant can help to establish a successful one. It is in simple things like personal support and organization that effective solutions to dyspraxia can be found. When you do this, you don't have to take complete control of their life. Of course the child needs to begin to take some responsibility for these things, because this is the way that they will need to approach the rest of their lives, but a little bit of help can show them the way.

Examinations

Formal assessment plays a huge part in education. We have different ways in which we register judgements about a child's abilities and you will be intimately involved in the preparation of dyslexic learners for assessment. Exam results are extremely influential, determining jobs, careers, education. Indeed, education symptoms are built upon examinations. They are the focal point for most of the teaching that any child receives, especially at this stage. Your job is to help the learner achieve results that confirm their abilities rather than reveal their dyspraxia.

The student who wants to succeed and feels positive because of the support they have received in school will be best placed to achieve in examinations.

The dyspraxic learner will need help to organize and to plan. This has to be a central message in everything to do with dyspraxics. They have difficulty in doing this, so teaching assistants need to get involved and help them. After all, the secret to examination success at any age lies in careful preparations. Here are some things that you can do:

- Help to create a timetable and a study programme in the run-up to the examinations.
- Draw up a timetable that includes a variety of activities. Shorter intense periods will be more productive than longer, less targeted sessions of revision for a student who finds concentration difficult.
- Encourage the use of highlighters to bring colour to the body of notes that has to be learned. Colours can be used to identify themes or issues. You can work these out together.
- Establish a set of internet resources to add variety and visual interest to revision.

Coursework is always going to play to the strengths of the dyspraxic student, especially in the age of computers. Dyspraxic students should be encouraged to achieve the highest marks possible in this element, which will compensate for any slight underachievement in time-determined situations. Sadly coursework may be slipping away because there are increasing problems with authenticity. In the digital world, written work can fly around the internet so swiftly. We live in a world where students can cut and paste their way to success. But for dyspraxic candidates we need to hang on to it for as long as we can.

You can help a great deal by providing a structure – a framework – for any coursework. Many people find it very difficult if they are presented with a blank sheet of paper. They need a framework, a way of breaking down a longer piece of work into smaller manageable sections.

Development activity 26: Coursework

Find a significant piece of examination coursework in a subject in which you feel confident.

Design a framework that will support a dyspraxic learner and enable them to achieve good results in the assignment.

Remember, your objective isn't to do the work for them but to make sure that they have a framework upon which they can design their own response.

- A teaching assistant should be fully involved in any field trips. You will be able to support the learner in an unfamiliar environment. It will also make sure that you are informed of the subject matter and are able to build upon it back in school. Keep parents informed too, because they could repeat the field trip at a later date if necessary.
- A teaching assistant needs to be fully aware of contemporary developments in study skills. These might involve relating knowledge to visual clues by designing word maps or spider diagrams. You can make tapes of revision material that can be played on a personal stereo. You can

record files onto a computer as MP3 files that can be played on MP3 players. Stay informed and involve yourself in any training the school might organize. Be ready to find and adapt revision aids.

Once you have developed the techniques required to help the dyspraxic student learn and revise, you need to help them structure their approach in the examination room.

A dyspraxic learner could approach exams with foreboding. The nature of examinations does not play to their strengths – the pressure to work quickly, to plan and organize, are precisely the things they have always needed help with. They may find it hard to deal with their own anxiety. They may find it hard to recall information in the correct order. They may struggle to write quickly and legibly. What they will need is a strategy for approaching the examination experience. Dyspraxia is not the sort of disadvantage that is going to give the learner access to your support in the examination room. The nature of the condition is that they are likely to be granted no more than extra time. So you will need to help them develop a strategy for the exam that will include this time, which generally is an additional 25 per cent.

- Ensure they have a revision plan and schedule written in diary form. 'Monday 5.00 pm – 6.00 pm history. 7.00 pm – 8.00 pm maths.'
- Break down revision into manageable chunks.
- Propose a plan to negotiate the entire exam. Indicate in which order questions should be attempted.
- Focus on how to use the available time. Specify how long should be spent on particular questions.
- Try to ensure that someone is there outside the examination room just to offer reassurance and to calm apprehensive students, A familiar face, telling everyone that the exam will be fine, no problem, can be important for everyone.

- A check can also be made that the necessary equipment has been brought.
- There is no reason why you shouldn't write out the time plan and display it at the front of the examination room for the benefit of everyone. So you could write '10.10 start question 2. 10.35 start question 3.'
- If appropriate, the school could provide dyspraxic candidates with a separate room, so that they will not be distracted by others and will have more success in maintaining their fragile concentration. Check with your examination officer.
- It is vital that examination invigilators are fully informed about the dyspraxic students and their entitlement to extra time. It is their duty to ensure that they get it.

Think for a moment . . .

Think about the calendar of events in your institution.

How frequent are the examinations?

When will the most challenging times of the year occur?

What impact will this programme have upon you?

How can you design a programme that will support dyspraxic learners?

Are there any particular strategies that you will need to implement?

13

18 and beyond

Like many young people, the dyspraxic student might view college and university with a sense of liberation. Finally they will be able to put behind them all their frustrations and forget the things that reminded them of their inadequacies and concentrate on what they *can* do. They can now make choices about what to do and how to do it.

The incidence of bullying should by now be in decline, though there will still be a residual lack of confidence as a result of a hard time at secondary school. By now there is less of a requirement to conform, as teenage lifestyle fractures into a whole host of possibilities. In the early part of secondary school everyone had to be the same. Now everyone wants to be different.

Some might be all too eager to leave school, where they have always confronted failure. But they need to be encouraged to think carefully about their options and you can play a really important role here. Dyspraxic learners shouldn't reject education too soon. After all, what sort of future will they have without it?

But of course it is never straightforward. Choices bring stressful interludes and the move towards greater independence can be haphazard. But leaving school is another change and it can be managed with help in the same way that other transitions are managed. Knowledge and preparation are the keys and you have a part to play. Support will be needed in filling in application forms and in preparing CVs, but this is normally offered to all students anyway. Dyspraxic students may need a number of attempts at it, but easy correction and revision is one of the familiar benefits of the electronic system that now processes applications. Once again, there must be an emphasis upon the transfer of information. Naturally this transition brings with it issues about self-support. All parents fret about this, but with dyspraxic students there are added concerns and important decisions to discuss.

- Is the student ready to leave home and deal with a new way of life?
- Can they deal with a new environment, with the need to form new relationships with students and tutors?
- Would the student benefit more from studying in their home town rather than moving away?
- Should the emphasis be upon somewhere that is easily accessible?

Most higher education institutes will have study advisers who will be available to assist students in their learning. I suppose these people fulfil an equivalent role to yourself. It might be good advice to suggest that your dyspraxic student makes contact with a study adviser soon after their arrival in order to make sure that their awareness is raised. It is a way of ensuring that the relevant information has indeed been passed on. No one can anticipate when it might be important.

All those stages that were required when the transfer was made between primary and secondary all those years ago need to be replayed, with the intention of developing familiarity with a new environment and the demands that it will make. The issues may be slightly different, that's all.

The dyspraxic student will need to find their way around this new space. It will all be unfamiliar and they might start bumping into things. Narrow aisles in libraries between shelves might be difficult places to manage. They might need to spend a lot of their time there.

They will also need to maintain their habit of making lists

and reminders. There is always the danger that they might miss appointments for seminars or they might forget about the milk in the fridge.

- Many students will need a timetable for changing and washing clothes.
- Not only dyspraxic students will find it difficult to start managing money. Can they remember not to go to the cash machine too often?
- Does the student have a filing system for storing notes so that they can be easily retrieved?
- Have they been sent away with birthday cards already addressed and labelled that merely need posting, so that they don't forget those important family milestones?

The need for careful organization has always been there. There will now be different things on those lists. All those things for which they previously relied upon others for help will become pressing issues when they become their own responsibility.

Teaching assistants can also help in the preparations for interviews, especially for the dyspraxic child who is not socially adept. It is inevitable that the inability to recognize facial expressions in a conversation or interview, the inability to maintain good eye contact or the shambling walk and slumped body shape, the weak handshake, will all give an impression that the student is not sociable. Immediately, inaccurate conclusions may be drawn. Of course, their clumsiness, their failure to pick up on clues in a conversation, will be less of a problem if the prospective institution has been made aware that this is a dyspraxic learner and knows to some extent what to expect. You would certainly wish to avoid any possibility of the dyspraxic student you have nurtured suddenly finding themselves unsupported in self-catering accommodation with a kettle and a Pot Noodle. So make sure they know. But at least in a liberal and learning atmosphere of a college or university you should be confident that they will receive a sympathetic welcome.

Further education is a huge thing for the family, and with a dyspraxic child the normal anxieties of a parent are magnified. They can see that this change in their child's life could be enormously beneficial and that it should happen. But they can't see how their child will be able to do it. A wide range of issues will consume the parent's fretful hours. The apprehension that parents feel could be allayed to some extent by ensuring that the institution acknowledges difficulties and gives some priority to ensure that accessible and suitable accommodation is available. Most places will try to ensure that those with more pressing needs are suitably supported. As always, the key here is effective communication between institutions. That has been shown to be important at every stage. You need to ensure that someone in your place is passing on the appropriate information. Families must take advantage of the open days organized by most further education institutions. Encourage your learner to do so. It is an excellent opportunity for them to familiarize themselves with this potential – and new – environment. They can model themselves there and meet equally confused and nervous students, apprehensive about an unfamiliar future.

At the same time, they can recognize the excitement of these future opportunities. It happens in a controlled and structured situation with parents in attendance. It is a gentle introduction and a good way of glimpsing the future. It is a vision of what the future can be and perhaps a spur to achievement.

Of course the dyspraxic student might not have a clue about what it will all mean. They may have wildly unrealistic expec-

Think for a moment . . .

Consider the anxieties a parent might feel when their dyspraxic child goes on to further education.

How could these anxieties be categorized?

What can you do to help resolve them?

tations of their own capabilities. Teach a dyspraxic a simple dish like a stir-fry with some noodles and suddenly in their eyes they have mastered all aspects of cooking. You, on the other hand (as it were), might retain that residual fear about whether they can slice things without losing a digit. But looking at accommodation and catering alternatives can provide a focus and an opportunity to engage, however casually, with a future that contains the cold reality of a pile of dirty underwear that needs immediate attention. To the usual teenage refusal to engage with what they see as irrelevant detail, you can add the emotional immaturity of dyspraxia. It is a murky cocktail indeed.

But parents need to stay practical and sensible expenditure on ready-sliced meat and veg from the supermarket can help. You have these ideas. You must share them. It is what a good teaching assistant has always done.

It can be a very worrying time, especially for a parent who has protected their child from the reality of domestic responsibilities. When a child's whole life might have been sustained by an imaginary world into which they have regularly retreated, then it can be difficult to get a focus on the essential details of living a semi-independent life: washing; ironing (OK, perhaps not); going to bed; getting up; bedding; sock management. All these are decisions that in the past they have been told not to make. Now who is there to make them? It will be enormously reassuring to parents if they come across someone like you who has already considered these difficulties and has some sensible and workable solutions.

Their ability to cope with others who might be less than sympathetic or who might wish to exploit them, for whatever reason, will always be a major concern. They will be awash with the same emotions as the rest of us, yet even less able to deal with them. What chance is there of them being able to be equal partners in a relationship? It seems to me that they usually react to events, as a consequence of the crucial delays that take place in their thought processes, but they are unable to control them or to take the initiative. This means that they will usually respond, rather than influence or direct, in most aspects of their life.

They will see going to university as a time to make new friends, perhaps a longed-for opportunity after so much difficulty at school, but they might not have the experience or the understanding of how to do it. They will need to plug themselves into a new network but they will probably have no one there to help them do it. Their response to those who show an interest in them can be too enthusiastic. Their ability to build friendships and to interpret others is thin. Years of being ridiculed or rejected can give them an air of desperation. And if they are going to find it hard to make relationships, how are they ever going to be able to end them?

We have all known people like this. It is all part of the emotional soup in which we live. We see their inept grasp of social skills and think little of it. We move on. Perhaps these people are undiagnosed dyspraxics. It is not our problem. But when that excruciating clumsiness in social situations that features in the work of many comedians is a reality for someone we love, then it stops being funny.

In the end, the dyspraxic child just seems so vulnerable. Both student and parents will require the support of someone who knows them. It might be the end of your relationship with a student who you have watched change and grow. As a professional you will want this final transition to be comfortable and successful. They should embrace these changes with your genuine approval. It will mean something to them.

Of course it is a big step. But it should be encouraged. None of us should ever accept the possibility of unfulfilled potential without a genuine and sustained struggle. If the dyspraxic student has the ability, then extending their studies will be the central part of their development as a person. What other opportunity will they ever have of leaving home and growing properly without it? Without it, what will they become?

14

In conclusion . . .

At some point, at whatever stage you are working, you will have to hand on your dyspraxic friend to someone else. What we want more than anything else is to hand them on so that they are ready to embrace new achievements. We all want to feel that we have played some part in their development and that their successes will continue and grow. The question is always: How do we measure success? This is a tricky issue, because even examination success is not really a reflection of anything other than the successful passing of exams. It doesn't tell us enough. It doesn't cast any light on whether or not the dyspraxic child has become a rounded and supportive personality. Even psychopaths are allowed to pass examinations.

I have thought long and hard about this. We all need to feel that what we do creates an impact, that we make a positive difference. This is particular the case with an issue as difficult and frustrating as dyspraxia. There will be so many setbacks, and so many times when progress appears to be minimal or insignificant. A teaching assistant must inevitably feel that they are irrelevant.

But a good teaching assistant shouldn't feel like that. Because the difference you will make will eventually be a great step made up of a lot of much smaller ones. This is why you need patience and resilience, because there is unlikely to be any great and unexpected transformation. Everything with dyspraxics is gradual, almost imperceptible. So keep on keeping on, and over time you will have made a huge difference.

But if we go back to this question that I posed, about how

you measure the success of what you do, I think that I have found a solution. It doesn't lie in data about performance or in externally verified tests. No, for most of you I have a much simpler measure: Does the dyspraxic learner come back to visit you after they have left your institution and moved on? OK, it may sound rather trivial, and it isn't scientific. But if you think about it, a dyspraxic student who stays in touch shows that:

- the relationship you established was important to them;
- they can make decisions and put them into action;
- they are confident enough to take the initiative for that visit. No one will have prompted them to do it. They have reflected upon their life and their obligations;
- they might well have had to make, and manage, travel arrangements;
- they want to share their successes and their news with you;
- they have a level of sophistication and social awareness;
- they have an awareness of obligations, perhaps also a sense of gratitude;
- it is not only their teachers they remember. It's the assistant who gave them so much;
- they are not afraid of revisiting their past.

A dyspraxic learner who never received the support that they did from you would be unlikely to act in this way. Your dyspraxic learner has grown.

And you have done something to change a life. Isn't that something that you can be justifiably proud of?

Think for a moment . . .

Consider who else might benefit from reading this book.

What are you going to tell them about it?

Which parts of it reflect your own experiences?